A
CALIFORNIAN'S
GUIDE TO THE
MAMMALS
AMONG US

Golden-mantled ground squirrel.

A
CALIFORNIAN'S
GUIDE TO THE
MAMMALS
AMONG US

Charles Hood

with photographs by Paul Carter, José G. Martínez-Fonseca,
John Haubrich, Fred Hood, and others

Heyday, Berkeley, California

Library of Congress Cataloging-in-Publication Data

Names: Hood, Charles, 1959- author. | Carter, Paul, 1966- photographer. | Martínez-Fonsesca, José, photographer. | Haubrich, John, photographer. | Hood, Fred, 1965- photographer.
Title: A Californian's guide to the mammals among us / Charles Hood ; with photographs by Paul Carter, José G. Martínez-Fonsesca, John Haubrich, Fred Hood, and others.
Description: Berkeley, California : Heyday, [2019] | Includes index. |
Identifiers: LCCN 2018042400 (print) | LCCN 2018054246 (ebook) | ISBN 9781597144711 (E-book) | ISBN 9781597144438 (pbk.)
Subjects: LCSH: Mammals--California--Identification.
Classification: LCC QL719.C2 (ebook) | LCC QL719.C2 H66 2019 (print) | DDC 599.09794--dc23
LC record available at https://lccn.loc.gov/2018042400

Cover Photo: Charles Hood
Cover and Interior Design/Typesetting: Ashley Ingram

Published by Heyday
P.O. Box 9145, Berkeley, CA 94709
(510) 549-3564
www.heydaybooks.com

Printed in East Peoria, Illinois, by Versa Press, Inc.

10 9 8 7 6 5 4 3 2 1

for Abbey...

...when I said my mammal list would stop at 500, oh, sorry—I meant to say 1,500.

Contents

This mountain lion cub is just six weeks old.

Introduction

Why Watch Animals?

Because animals do interesting things. Because they come in so many shapes and sizes. Because they are everywhere. Because it's fun. Because why not.

A full-racked elk, majestic at sunrise? How cool is that? You don't even have to go to Yellowstone: this shot is from Del Norte Coast Redwoods State Park, south of Crescent City. Or what about sea otters? They are super easy to see *and* they are cool *and* there's a brink-of-extinction backstory, so bonus points all around. Use rocks as tools. Thickest fur of any mammal. They sleep wrapped in kelp while holding hands. And they are utterly silent: unlike your neighbor's dog (or the ninety-decibel coquí frog, coming to a garden near you), sea otters will never wake you up at night.

Less well known, kangaroo rats are easy to find in Joshua Tree and Death Valley and other desert parks, and even on the chaparral hillsides near Hemet. Nicknamed k-rats, they are bouncing, skittering balls of cuteness with tails twice as long as their bodies. They can jump eight feet and go months without water. The state has not one, not three, not six, but thirteen different kinds of kangaroo rat, making California a world hotspot for this fascinating group of animals.

Mammals fill our dreams and myths. From trickster tales about Coyote to Aesop's fable of the tortoise and the hare, we experience a reality mediated by animal stories. (North America has half a dozen native hares—we call ours jackrabbits.) Words like "bear," "wolf," "beaver," and "otter" date back at least 8,000 years, to the earliest Indo-European roots. At cave-art sites like Lascaux and Chauvet in France, bison and horses gallop past, hunted by cave lions and human handprints. The realism astounds us even now. In Namibia's Brandberg Mountain Range, caves preserve 20,000-year-old antelope paintings that still glow vivid and fresh today, and in Little Petroglyph Canyon near Ridgecrest, cliffs and boulders display herds of bighorn sheep carved into the patina of the rock. The people who made these were gifted (and persistent) artists but also were astute observers of the natural world. Cave art preserves our first field guides.

What does all this animal art mean? We're not sure, but everybody agrees it means *something*. As art critic John Berger suggests, "Animals first entered the imagination as messengers and promises."

Bighorn sheep dance across basalt near Ridgecrest.

The good news with mammals is that we are experts right out of the gate. Birdwatching requires a long apprenticeship and pricey binoculars in order to advance up the tiers, but as mammals ourselves we have been studying our own kind all our lives. Even a toddler is already an ace mammal watcher, able to know at a glance if Mom is angry or in the mood to be generous with vanilla wafers or perhaps so distracted that now is the perfect opportunity to investigate that mysterious bag of treasures, her purse.

Of all the images that make our world, animal images are particularly buried inside us. We feel the pull of them before we know to name them, or how to even fully see them.

—Elena Passarello

Puzzle Solvers Unite

Another reason to take up mammal watching has to do with how much remains to be investigated and explained. Even more so than birding, every mammal trip is a potential voyage of discovery. The pallid bat is pale yellow and doesn't hunt mosquitoes the way most other North American bats do. Instead, it catches scorpions and insects right on the ground (see page 78.) That much everybody had agreed on. Recently somebody was studying cactus in Baja and realized that pallid bats eat cardon cactus fruit too, and in fact, as they start eating, they crawl all the way inside the fruit to gorge themselves. Nobody had a clue that the scourge of scorpion and centipede had such a sweet tooth, or that it seems to be beneficial to the cactus—this bat species may turn out to be an important cactus pollinator.

From wolverines to foxes, a thousand questions remain. For example, we are still finding new species of whales. The first intact specimens of the spade-toothed whale came from a mother and calf that stranded on a beach in New Zealand in 2010. Before that, the species was known only from a piece of jawbone from 1872 and a scrap of skull from the 1950s. Indeed, as field guide author and natural history illustrator Fiona Reid says, when it comes to mammals, we are in an era exploding with possibility. "Because there's still so much to explore, mammal watching is a constant parade of surprises. That's so exciting. There is a lot left to do."

Fiona Reid and Micah Riegner looking for new species.

Many outdoor pursuits need major investments in equipment, long drives to get to the kayak put-in or trailhead, or lessons, guides, and certification. Not so with animals: mammal study can be one of the simplest, quietest hobbies. One enthusiast calls her daily mammal strolls "walking meditation." Indulging in a meandering ramble, scanning for raccoon tracks in the creek bank, stopping to photograph a yearling deer, noting the dash-and-peer burst of a squirrel—these are all ways to get out of our own heads and connect with a wider environment. As an extension of that, it doesn't even need to be a long walk: sometimes the best way to experience wildlife is just to sit quietly and let things come to us. As John Muir liked to remind guests in Yosemite, "People ought to saunter in the mountains—not hike!"

The bench says it all—The Forest of Nisene Marks, Santa Cruz.

A final idea about mammal watching centers on an old-fashioned word: "joy." We don't celebrate this concept very much, yet perhaps we should. You'll certainly give yourself a better chance of experiencing the sublime and the magnificent by being out in nature than you ever will lining up for the drive-thru at Starbucks or sitting through previews in the multiplex.

For example, if one takes the boat from Ventura over to Santa Cruz Island to see the endemic fox, the cross-channel boat ride often intersects pods of common dolphins. Numbers seem magical: you can be surrounded by 1,000; 2,000; or even 3,000 dolphins at once, adults and babies, all of them leaping and splashing and bow riding, a great dance of some of California's most attractive animals and a show that gets everybody on board oohing and aahing and reaching for phones and cameras.

Other boat trips can be just as lucky. This photo of a Risso's dolphin was taken in Monterey barely ten minutes from the dock. There was a pod of seventy-five feeding and socializing dolphins, so close to the boat one could hear the *spiff* of their breath as they came to the surface. Filled with the spirit of the day, one dolphin kept geysering up to the surface and crashing down with a backward splash, over and over. The exuberance was undeniable. Such an encounter is a joyous moment indeed, the kind of experience one hopes will last for hours.

Eight deer on the slope
in the summer morning mist.
The night sky blue.
Me like a mare let out to pasture.
—Linda Gregg

What Is a Mammal?

All mammals have hair, even whales and naked mole rats. Most bear live young (excluding a few egg-layers in Australia), and all mammals nurse young with milk. There are some common skeletal features in terms of middle ear bones and fused jawbones, but otherwise, that's about it. You have the same number of neck vertebrae as a giraffe and the same size of brain as a dolphin. Your hand and a bat's wing are basically the same thing; their hands just have longer, thinner bones and a membrane of skin stretched tautly between them like the fabric of a kite.

We've been around a long time, or at least our ancestors have. Protomammals coexisted with dinosaurs and witnessed the same earth-shattering comet strike 66 million years ago. Fortunately for us, some of them made it through the Cretaceous–Paleogene extinction event and so here we all are now, smiling and waving like prom queens. Despite the commonly used expression *survival of the fittest*, a better way of saying it might be *survival of the most adaptable* or even *survival of the luckiest*. A few lightning strikes one way or the other and instead of the golden age of mammals, the planet now could be celebrating the golden age of salamanders and dragonflies.

ring finger

middle finger

pointer finger

pinky

thumb

elbow

The human hand shares the same structure as the wings of bats. This tropical species, the greater fishing bat, hunts for fish as well as insects.

Yet survive we did, with species radiating out to fill niches from the Arctic to Baja. Most estimates put the mammal species total somewhere between 5,500 and 6,500, including at least 450 primates and more than 1,400 bats, some smaller than a silver dollar. The differences in the final totals depend on whether one is a splitter (cutting the apple into ever finer slices) or a lumper (fewer items overall, defined by more inclusive boundaries). Careers are at stake in making these distinctions, and funding too, as well as how one justifies conservation work politically, so the "species question" becomes messy quickly. It is nearly as hard to be sure about species totals as it is to decide how many science-fiction films have ever been released, or how many Hello Kitty

Facts sometimes have a strange and bizarre power that makes their inherent truth seem unbelievable.
—Werner Herzog

products are out there. (What counts as science fiction, how many minutes does something have to run to be a "film," and what does "released" mean—uploaded to YouTube and seen by three people?) Bar fights have been started over smaller questions than these.

With world mammals, one thing that all parties do agree about is that not everything is cataloged and known: almost certainly dozens (even hundreds) more mammal species remain to be discovered. We probably have all the bats in California sorted out, but the key word is "probably." Further work may reveal more species, based perhaps on citizen science data—maybe even on recordings or photographs provided by the readers of this book.

California's Mammal Cornucopia

Move over, Alaska; take a backseat, Texas: at its current tally of 220 species, California's mammal list is the largest of any US state. (It's larger in fact than the list for all of Canada.) That's because a long coastline gives us access to an ocean's worth of whales and dolphins, and on shore, with so many habitats, we have room for generalists (raccoons, skunks), specialists (shrews best adapted to lush, wet coastal redwood forests), and altitude-restricted residents, like the yellow-bellied marmot, a large alpine squirrel that is related to woodchucks (the animal featured in the movie *Groundhog Day*). The marmot weighs eleven pounds and has an alarm call so loud it sounds like a ground squirrel testing a megaphone.

Marmots like rocky slopes near alpine meadows; look for them in summer around Mineral King, Tioga Pass, and Lake Tahoe.

Birders have a competition called a big day, when a team goes out for twenty-four hours and tries to check off as many species as possible. Usually routes are scouted beforehand, so the teams know what roosts where, and they schedule accordingly. The mammal big days that have taken place in California have been more ad hoc; there is less competitive pressure, and the locations of animals can't be predicted so easily. Even so, folks have come up with lists of over forty species in one day. You would have a hard time topping that even on an African safari.

"This town is infested with squirrels, have you noticed?"
"I'd rather say it's rich *with squirrels."*
—*Elizabeth McKenzie,* The Portable Veblen

To put this in perspective, Holly Faithfull is a British guide who leads wildlife tours all over the world. She loves bringing clients to California, many of whom are "gobsmacked by the diversity." She adds, "How lucky you are in California. You might even see a puma when you're driving home from work."

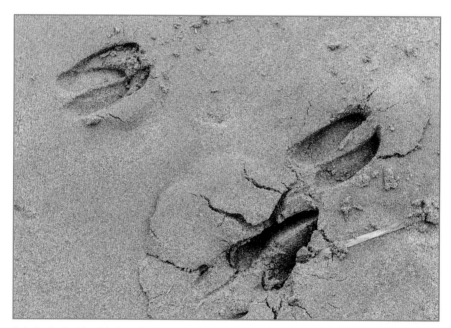

Mule deer tracks at low tide, Morro Bay.

These charcoal kilns in Death Valley once supported ore smelting. Now they host woodrat nests.

The spade-toothed whale mentioned earlier has never been seen alive...*yet.* Maybe you'll be the first person to see one.

Natives versus Exotics

Does it matter where things come from? Some birdwatchers don't like house sparrows and starlings because they are not native; bluebirds were here all along, but pigeons first came with European settlement, and for some bird spotters, pedigree matters. They won't count certain species on their lists, and most ornithology grad students would rather study native puffins than introduced parrots.

The fact is the interface between wild and non-wild has become ever more porous. Coyotes forage in cities now in ways that are obviously human-influenced, and because we killed off all the grizzlies, now black bears can live in the mountains of Southern California—habitat they were previously excluded from when the bigger, badder grizzly still was in charge. Not having grizzlies makes it safer for us to camp and hike, and it also means black bears flourish in ways they didn't two hundred years ago. Take away one thing, another thing fills its place. That said, on average, non-native species cause more harm than good.

In an effort to accept the world as it is (not how it should be), this book includes species that are native elsewhere and have been intentionally released here: the Virginia opossum for example, or eastern fox squirrels. Other animals are also present in our landscapes thanks to humans, though perhaps more incidentally than intentionally, including feral cats and the European boar, also called feral pig. For better or worse, they too are mammals among us.

The fox squirrel is a non-native species, originally from the East Coast and now widespread in parks and backyards.

Island foxes on Santa Cruz Island are supposed to be wild, but careless backpackers reward the bold and the curious with tasty snacks.

Are we glad or sad that feral camels don't graze side by side with desert mustangs? Urban legend says that after the failed attempt to create a camel corps at Fort Tejon in the 1850s, the leftover stock was sold to traders and mule skinners, and those camels had baby camels, and some got loose, and ghost camel sightings lasted the next hundred years. They would have been both Bactrian camels (the two-humped kind) and dromedaries (one-humped), though sadly the stories probably are not true.

And yet a circus elephant once got stuck in the La Brea Tar Pits, and on-the-lam zoo flamingos have lived for years in the Salton Sea. One winter somebody's pet tiger survived a month outside Los Angeles before it was shot by deputies in a ravine near an elementary school. All that time it had been living off of wild game the same as any puma, though perhaps alarming even the mountain lions by leaving behind muddy paw prints big as dinner plates.

Since humans first huddled around campfires, stories have been told of wild horses with wind in their manes, fire in their eyes, and freedom in their hearts. Those horses eluded capture, and scorned the comforts of civilization.

—Terri Farley

Outlaw bands of feral camels in the Mojave Desert? Stranger things have happened.

Albino Bats, Black Bobcats, and Blue Spirit Bears

Here's a fancy word: "pelage." It is for mammals what plumage is to birds—the outer covering, the fur or coat or pelt. Some animals, such as mule deer, have very consistent, reliable, unvarying pelage. Each deer is mostly the same color as the one next to it. T'ain't no such thing as an Appaloosa mule deer.

A few animals, like snowshoe hares, molt into separate winter and summer coats, white and brown; other times, illness or injury or mud can alter appearance. Other species vary individual to individual naturally—black bears can be cinnamon brown or even blond, and in British Columbia the palest form is called a spirit bear. Bobcats are usually sandy brown but in the eastern US once in a great, great while they show a dark color phase, sort of a "black panther" bobcat. Darker than usual is called melanistic; in most mammals there can be pale individuals as well, or even true albinos, which lack all pigment.

What this means is that sometimes you'll see something that just doesn't look right. The structure will be familiar, even if outside packaging is a bit queer. With good notes, usually you can figure out even the oddest pattern, though a few sightings just have to be entered into the question mark side of the ledger.

This recently photographed bat is an albino, the first documented instance of this for this species.

Fieldcraft

When trying to see animals, being quiet and still matters more than the brand of binoculars or which shade of khaki your shirts claim to be. The naturalist Fiona Reid notes that mammals "appear to be less threatened by humans if they remain motionless." She explains, "By standing absolutely still, not only have I had good views of animals as they walked close by me, but I have had a northern tamandua [a small anteater] step on my feet and start to climb my legs, a variegated squirrel jump onto my head from a fence post, and a paca [a rainforest guinea pig] sniff my shoes."

Every tree invites the wind.
—Gary Soto

Ralph Waldo Emerson invented the term "bird-while," meaning the amount of time that a bird will let you study it. That bird-while can stretch to half an hour, depending on the critter and if you're quiet and patient. Anything is possible: I never expected to see a ringtail in the wild, let alone get its picture, but as page 100 proves, patience (and luck) can pay big dividends. Even something as common as mule deer in Yosemite are easier to study (and photograph) as long as everybody doesn't start waving and pointing, with the loudest person shouting, "Over HERE, over HERE, WOW, come look at this!!" When that starts happening, even the rocks and trees probably wish they could run away.

How to See Mammals During the Day

It's normal to think we need to go to a national park (or the zoo) to see a lot of animals, but mostly it's about habit of mind—sort of. The more you look, the more you'll see.

I recently visited the headquarters of the Santa Clara Valley Audubon Society at McClellan Ranch in Cupertino, near where Highway 85 crosses I-280. This South Bay preserve is small yet charming. Native walnut trees shade Stevens Creek and fenced plots preserve community gardens; one can listen for Nuttall's woodpeckers or wait for chestnut-backed chickadees to zip down and investigate the bird feeders.

I mainly wanted to photograph birds; mammals were not on my agenda. Yet driving to the park, just as I got off the freeway I was surprised to see a Virginia opossum cross the road and disappear down a storm drain. "Hey little guy, you're out late—a hawk's gonna find you!" Arriving at the parking lot I had hardly gotten my binoculars out when pointed ears and a loping gait made me look up and smile. A coyote was crossing the field—no, two coyotes, going home to their den. Following them I flushed six mule deer, which had been bedding down illicitly in the garden plots, able to sneak into this vegetable buffet thanks to a broken fence.

- **Never approach, feed, chase, or harm any wild animal.**
- **Keep dogs on a leash and small children close to you.**
- **If you see a rattlesnake, stay away and notify park staff, (408) 777-3120.**
- **If you see a mountain lion, stay away and notify the Sherriff's Department, (408) 299-3211 or dial 911 in case of an emergency.**

If You Encounter a Mountain Lion:

Face the lion. Back away slowly.

Make yourself large. Shout.

Keep children close. Lift them up without bending over.

If Attacked, Fight Back

As the morning warmed up, the first ground squirrels came out, as did fox squirrels, bushy-tailed and agile, scampering up and down the oak trunks. Checking the 4-H livestock pens, I noticed small black droppings that revealed a mouse had been looking for grain, while on the community notice board, posters explained what to do if you came across a mountain lion.

All this nature can be found very close to homes and schools and freeways, in the middle of a huge urban area. To see animals you don't have to go to Yosemite or Anza-Borrego—though they're great places. Our everyday neighborhoods are home to wildlife too.

How to See Mammals After Dark

Here's where the real fun begins—going out after dark with flashlights, or driving back roads with a spotlight, hoping to catch a bit of eyeshine. If you've ever seen

a flash-lit photo of people with demonic red eyes, you know that eyes adapted to see in the dark reflect light back when a light source hits them. In animals usually they glow yellow or green, and looking for animals after dark is called spotlighting. On a safari it can be called doing a night drive—the terms mean the same thing. You even can spotlight from a boat.

This Botta's pocket gopher was photographed on a residential street in the heart of Los Angeles.

When walking trails at night, always have a backup in case the first light runs out of juice. Most people use a headlamp plus a handheld light. (Note that most British birders call a flashlight a torch, a term used in Africa, Europe, and sometimes Latin America.)

Anecdotal evidence suggests that moonless nights are the most productive, under the theory that predation by owls and badgers makes smaller things hesitant to go far from the burrow on evenings flooded by moonlight. This may or may not be true; the kangaroo rat that opened this section was photographed on a night of a full moon, and one never can guess how one's luck will run. What is true is that moonless nights give one a chance to enjoy the Milky Way. The darkest of California's "dark sky" locations are worth visiting just to see the amazing parade of stars.

As an activity, spotlighting works best as a team project. One person drives slowly while the shotgun-seat passenger leans out the open window (seatbelt latched, of course), sweeping the hillsides or open desert with the spotlight. If you catch eyeshine, slow down and work as a team to identify the deer or cow or badger or whatever it is out there in the dark. Night birds like barn owls and poorwills can be seen this way too.

Even insects have eyeshine, as these tropical moths reveal.

Common sense required: don't light up houses, oncoming traffic, or police cars. Spotlighting from cars is not allowed inside national parks.

Other ways to document animals at night include setting up a trail camera—this is especially interesting if you live a bit outside of town and have animal paths on your property—and using handheld bat detectors that plug into your smart phone. They use bats' echolocation patterns to reveal species, the way that

Night, when words fade and things come alive.
—Antoine de Saint-Exupéry

specific birdsong tells us a field is full of meadowlarks and lark sparrows, even when we can't see them.

Keeping a List

Birders keep lists and some mammal watchers do too. As with anything—a runner's mileage log or index cards for every movie you've seen—over time the accumulated total might surprise you. An October weekend in Monterey could launch a list with ten species fairly easily—mule deer and fox squirrels in the Pacific Grove cemetery, raccoons and bats after dark by Crespi Pond, sea otters and harbor seals and sea lions as you leave the harbor on a half-day whale-watching boat, dolphins and whales as you motor farther out to sea. (Boats make you seasick? You can see gray whales from land at Point Vicente, in Southern California, and many other headlands. I've even kayaked with them inside Newport Harbor, and seen them from the beach at Gaviota State Park.)

Keeping an eye out for new mammals can add interest to any outing. North of Mono Lake, the ghost town of Bodie hosts pika colonies in the mining scree. Pikas are pint-sized relatives of rabbits that usually stick to the talus slopes of alpine meadows. You wouldn't expect them in the high desert next to a derelict gold mine, yet there they are.

Bodie State Park preserves a ghost town and is a place to see golden-mantled ground squirrels and least chipmunks right in the parking lot.

New species for your list are probably closer than you would guess. Brush rabbits—a different species from regular cottontails—can be seen by UC Irvine at San Joaquin Marsh or even adjacent to Highway 1, in the parking lot for kayakers at Moss Landing. The picture of a white-tailed antelope squirrel on page 30 was

All lists start in litany, as prayers.
The pleasure is the invention.

—*Robert Hass*

taken in a front yard in Trona, a mining town named by some skeptics as the most depressed (and depressing) town in California. One night after a wedding reception in Bolinas I saw three gray foxes in ten minutes. The animals are out there...once we start looking.

The brush rabbit is only found in coastal California; it is smaller than the usual desert cottontail.

How to Use This Book

The table of contents is organized in taxonomic order, meaning it follows the scientific consensus for what's related to what, arranged from eldest lineages to more recent. This tree-of-life approach is shared by most field guides; in any list for a national park, you can expect to find the opossum entry first, well before bear or fox. Bats usually come about the middle. If you can't find something, the index cross-references every animal mentioned anywhere in the book.

The promise of any field guide is that you can name all the beasts in field and forest. We hope this book helps you do that. But a secondary purpose here is to celebrate the diversity all around us, whether or not you can ID every mouse or track down every shrew. The main pleasure is just to go out looking in the first place.

Let's put on our hats and sunscreen and get started.

Virginia Opossum _Didelphis virginiana_

Originally native to the eastern US and Mexico, the opossum first came to California in 1910. Although the full name is Virginia opossum, in North America there's just the one, so most people drop the state title. The word "opossum" is Algonquian; the initial _o_ is usually (but not always) silent.

With its snouty front and waddling gait, the opossum's motto is _Beauty is in the eye of the beholder_. To some it looks like a rat, especially since it is nocturnal and silvery gray, but the opossum is larger, slower, and basically odder—no wood mouse or sewer rat has that half-mean, half-puzzled white face. Croplands, marshes, exurbia, ditches: it's at home in all of these, other than that it doesn't venture high into the Sierra Nevada or thrive in true deserts. The long, naked tail helps it grasp tree limbs, so opossums are as likely to be seen using power lines as a Tarzan highway as they are to turn up investigating your compost bins.

As a generalist omnivore, the opossum can eat more or less anything, from carrion to carrots to cat food. It is a marsupial, so mama has a pouch, and the bean-sized babies instinctually climb up to it as soon as they are born; but for an opossum, survival of the fittest starts early. No matter how many young are born (up to twenty), mom only averages thirteen mammary attachment points total. Sorry, guys: first come, first served. Another curiosity is that opossums are highly resistant to both rabies and rattlesnake venom. They have not just opposable thumbs but opposable toes (making them super good climbers); and the male opossum has a forked ("bifurcated") penis. An early folktale had it that he impregnated the gal opossum through her nose, but it's more about the plug fitting the socket: his equipment is shaped like that to match the female's side of the equation.

Can opossums "play possum"? Indeed so. When faced with a threat they go stiff and glassy-eyed, sometimes foaming at the mouth and grimacing to show their fifty teeth, while anal glands can release a power-ful, death-stench smell. This semi-comatose state can last for hours. Opossums are defensive players only, and while they'll hiss ferociously if cornered, they usually never attack people. And just to prove that

I'm hoping to be astonished tomorrow by I don't know what.
—*Jim Harrison*

nothing is too obscure to have a fan club, somewhere out there is the National Opossum Society, plus a second group, the Opossum Society of the United States. Most animals have a collective noun, like a pride of lions or a pod of whales; for a gang of opossums the term is "passel." What would be a good word for a gathering of opossum fans—a feign of them? A doze? "A somnolence of opossum club members was seen in the hotel lobby, all wearing matching gray coats."

In the wild the opossum lifespan is short, usually just a few years, and nomadic as well: they make temporary nests but usually move on in a few days or weeks. Abundant in all of our urban areas, opossums mostly try to stay out of sight and out of the way.

If you've not yet seen one—and sorry, but this is a bit morbid—watch local roadkill, because that's a good way to tell if you have opossums in your neighborhood. You almost certainly do, and probably many more nocturnal species as well.

Human Beings, People, Mankind *Homo sapiens*

North America's only native primate is a bilaterally symmetrical biped widely distributed in all habitats. It's not hard to find: most of the population clusters within a hundred miles of the coast, with secondary concentrations at river deltas and desert oases. Juveniles and outliers disperse widely and unpredictably, however, and solo humans can be found rowing far off the coast, skylining the Sierra crest, or jauntily traversing saline desert valleys, whistling a tune.

With sharp binocular vision, *Homo sapiens* sees in depth and in saturated color; humans also dream in color and use color to organize the world into categories, including a lot of malarkey about race. George Orwell once said a human being is just a bag for pouring food into, yet from that same mouth the human voice spans three octaves, from coos and churrs to yodels, howls, and Axl Rose crescendos. Daily vocabulary centers on a core of 3,000 words, with another 20,000 known and read by early adolescence. Tool use is facilitated by a problem-solving brain, ambidextrous hands, and multisectioned arms with elastic, rotating joints. If this were a new model of robot, people would line up around the block to have one.

> Rats and roaches live by competition under the laws of supply and demand; it is the privilege of human beings to live under the laws of justice and mercy.
> —*Wendell Berry*

When did humans first arrive in California? There must be a before/after divide, but we can't decide where to put it. Human remains on Santa Rosa Island

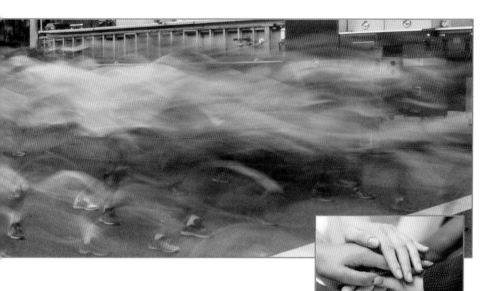

date from 13,000 years ago, but genetic markers suggest humans crossed from Asia to North America much earlier than that. Were these visitors traveling on foot or by boat? Did founding populations expand incrementally or hopscotch across the map? What motivated them—fear, hunger, curiosity, joy? They had to know it was a new world since even the jays were different, but how did that newness make them feel? So many questions, so few answers.

A family reunion would need to include a lot of our cousins: worldwide, there are 450 other primates, from gorillas to baboons to marmosets, and genetically we're all nearly identical. Why are we at the top of the pile and not any of them? One recent paper argues that humans are such successful primates because we have a "unique ecological plasticity"—we are very good at adapting every time situations change. After humans, the planet's next most abundant large mammal is the crabeater seal of Antarctica, a flannel-gray pinniped with an odd smile and blubbery pelt. It lives on pack ice and eats krill. The total crabeater seal population may number 10- or perhaps even 50 million individuals—another fact of nature we're not quite sure about.

If we surveyed the other members of the animal kingdom, they probably would vote for more seals and fewer people.

Black-Tailed Jackrabbit and White-Tailed Jackrabbit *Lepus californicus* and *Lepus townsendii*

Jackrabbits take their names from their donkey-tall ears (as in, "jackass rabbit"); everywhere else in the world they're just called hares. Two kinds live here: the black-tailed jackrabbit, found in deserts and scrubby brushland up into the forest belt, and the white-tailed jackrabbit, which is rare and found around Mono Lake. You can tell them apart by tail color and range. Both of these are bigger than rabbits, with longer legs, taller ears, and even wilder, more explosive giddy-ups. *Bang*: when the starter's pistol goes off, jackrabbits bust loose like a bronco on crank, leaping and twisting and eating up the creosote at forty-five miles an hour. The last thing most hikers see is a puff of dust as the jackrabbit disappears over the horizon.

Sadly, despite being the star of postcards, dude ranches, and dive bars everywhere, the so-called "jackalope" is a taxidermist's hoax. It has a jackrabbit's body topped by spritely antlers. No such animal really exists—insert long sigh here.

Hares don't hibernate (nor do rabbits), but in summer in Death Valley the jackrabbit needs to wait out the heat of the day and does so resting in an

Left and above: Black-tailed jackrabbit.

Black-tailed jackrabbit: You can't see me!

above-ground scrape. The raisin-sized droppings are dark when fresh, and they weather into small yellow balls; especially in the desert you can tell when jackrabbits have been hanging out just from all the petrified pellets. Who's the buffest jackrabbit of all? Only one way to find out. In spring the males box over females, a manic jig that gives us the expression *crazy as a March hare*.

Born completely furred and with eyes open, a baby jackrabbit is called a leveret. If you want to show off a bit, explain to your friends that a male hare is called a jack and a female is a jill, as opposed to rabbits, where the adult male is a buck and the female is a doe. The collective noun for hares is drove, though one also may speak of a band of hares, a leap of hares, or a kindle of hares. Rabbits in a herd would be called a bevy, though calling them a down of rabbits has ardent fans too. In Australia, where the introduced European rabbit is a great pest, the correct term would be a plague of rabbits.

*Concrete is heavy; iron is hard—
but the grass will prevail.
—Edward Abbey*

The European hare of art and fable has been introduced into parts of North and South America, usually with poor results for everything besides the hare. Other than as escaped pets, that hare species does not occur in California—at least not yet.

Desert Cottontail and Brush Rabbit

Sylvilagus audubonii and *Sylvilagus bachmani*

From Easter candy to Bugs Bunny, here's one animal everybody knows. True, headlights confuse them—as with jackrabbits, they seem determined to zag and zig right into our tires—but an abundance of rabbits is good news for bobcats, hawks, coyotes, and hungry snakes, plus of course ravens and crows and turkey vultures, who swoop down to clean up the leftovers. Rabbits were once a primary game animal for Native Americans and were caught in communal drives (and then dispatched with a boomerang-like killing stick), or else were hunted with bows and blunt-tipped arrows. Slings and snares were used as well, as were trained dogs. The meat became supper, and the fur became clothing and blankets; and also (according to one ethnographer), dried rabbit toes, strung with beads on necklaces, "once served as Miwok love charms."

The most common species, desert cottontail, gets the name half right. "Cottontail," yes, they've got that, and they do live in the desert; but they are common in brushier habitat as well, occurring in fields, orchards, nature reserves, and scrublands from San Diego to San Francisco, and up both sides of the Sierra. In the greater West it can be found from Montana to Texas. It is a successful package: tall ears detect creeping enemies (and radiate surplus heat); the fur is basically

the color of scrub; and when they are spotted, powerful hind legs burst into escape mode like Usain Bolt launching from the starting blocks. Another name for this species is Audubon's

Each species is a masterpiece, a creation assembled with extreme care and genius.

—E. O. Wilson

The brush rabbit (top left) prefers to stay under cover. Its ears are smaller than the cottontail's, and the underside of its tail is gray, not white. Above, left, and opposite, the desert cottontail is the expected species in most of California. Both species have small ears when young.

Mountain cottontail is an animal of sagebrush and juniper; its ears don't have black tips. Look for it around Mono Lake.

cottontail; you can see it day and night, but prime times are dawn and dusk.

Shyer, smaller, and more nocturnal and chaparral dependent, the brush rabbit can be told from the desert cottontail by size, habitat, and a mostly dark (not fluffy white) tail. It is found west of the Sierra, overlapping with what botanists call the California Floristic Province. Think manzanita and toyon berry: if you're in sight of those communities, you've probably found the native range of brush rabbits.

In the Sierra, the snowshoe hare looks like a rabbit but is a different genus and the fur turns white in winter. Look for it along alder-lined streams or in high meadows. In transition, the fur can be half brown, half white, as the sun (to paraphrase John Muir) melts winter snow into spring music.

Do rabbits breed like rabbits? The brush rabbit has a chaste average of two litters per annum, but the desert cottontail can have up to seven litters in one year. At first the babies are naked and blind, but they grow quickly, and rabbits are sexually mature by ten months. Well, they probably need to be: the world is a cruel and sharp-edged place, and all those coyotes out there have a den full of mouths to feed. Yet the rabbits, like the plants themselves, come back each spring. Richard Adams, *Watership Down*: "A foraging wild creature, intent above all upon survival, is as strong as the grass."

Western Gray Squirrel *Sciurus griseus*

Bounding and bushy-tailed, the western gray is our native tree squirrel, expected in Sierra oaks and pines but also following cool weather and mossy conifers down to the Monterey and redwood coasts. They also like native black oaks and walnut groves, so extend into the Sacramento floodplain. In the novel *The Portable Veblen*, Elizabeth McKenzie gets it exactly right when she says of one that its "topcoat was charcoal, its chest white as an oxford shirt, its tail rakish as the feather in a conquistador's cap." Squirrels are easy to love, yet one person's pet soon becomes the next person's pestilence: the "western" part of the name separates it from the eastern gray squirrel, native to the other half of North American but much cursed in the UK, where it has caused declines in their native red squirrel species.

We only have a few eastern grays here in California, but we do have lots and lots of the non-native eastern fox squirrel, cinnamon backed and urban; it is featured in the following entry. In comparison, the gray squirrel is all-gray (not blended with yellow) and has a clean white belly. Which one lives where is not exactly a clean divide: you can see both western gray and fox squirrels side by side in Henry Cowell Redwoods State Park, inland from Santa Cruz, and in Griffith Park near Hollywood.

Gray squirrels eat acorns, pine seeds, flower buds, mushrooms, and truffles, and they are active year-round, thanks in part to scatter hoarding. That phrase means what's buried for later is randomized; it contrasts with larder hoarding, which is when an animal defends a central cache. The brainiac gray squirrel has spatial memory any human would envy, and they can remember the locations of hundreds of food stashes through the whole forest. Do they ever leave a few behind? Yes, and you can tell exactly where: some squirrel's lost acorn is now an adult tree.

They signal danger and express annoyance with their tails and also can chuck and squeak with ferocious intent. Squirrels maintain not territories, but social position backed by physical dominance, and so the top males dash after rivals or patrol for females in heat, always at full tilt. Gal squirrels chase too, saying, "So, you think you're able to keep up with me, lover boy? We'll just see about that." Once they have courted, the actual encounter lasts less than a minute. In the animal world version of a chastity belt, the gent then seals off the female's vagina with a waxy plug, hoping to keep his sperm in and that of his rivals out.

I can no more explain why I like "natural history"
than why I like California canned peaches.
—Theodore Roosevelt

Our other native squirrels include the Douglas squirrel—small, dark, and Spock-eared—and the strictly nocturnal flying squirrel, which stretches floppy skin tight to glide between trees. If near one in the dark, you'll hear it land with a muffled splat, as if somebody just missed you with a fastball of compacted snow. In a cage a flying squirrel is colored soft gray, but it seems brighter if spotted by flashlight or in headlights. According to Vladimir Dinets, a flying squirrel seen from the car "looks like a fast-flying white paper envelope."

Another tree-lover, the Douglas squirrel, is smaller and redder than the gray squirrel and has pale eye crescents and pointy ears.

Eastern Fox Squirrel *Sciurus niger*

Originally native to the eastern United States, the fox squirrel now claims all parks, backyards, and urban forests as its own, using power lines as highways and happily sampling everything from native acorns to the most exotic fruits of the Amazon jungle. If we grow it, cook it, or throw it away, this squirrel can find a way to eat it.

It is more brightly orange than the western gray squirrel, and much more likely to be found inside the city than along the mountain trail. In their home states they show a variety of color phases including black and white, but all of the ones in California look like the fox squirrels found in Tennessee, meaning they are a grizzled blend of tan, cream, gray, and cinnamon. They were introduced in the 1890s to San Francisco, in the early 1900s in Los Angeles, and by the 1920s in San Diego. Initially conditions must have been a bit rough—we are lusher, more varied now—but they survived and now fill the urban corridors from Balboa Park to Sacramento, spreading a few miles more each year.

Although trees are their happy places, fox squirrels also feed on the ground, looking for nuts, trash, or fallen fruit, but unlike ground squirrels, when they're alarmed they scoot straight up the nearest tree, even the floss silk tree with its spine-studded bark. (In contrast, startled ground squirrels always dash for a burrow, patch of brush, or the shade of a nearby car.) They are not especially social or communal, but they do keep in touch vocally, and they are usually easy to see all day long.

Attention Squirrels!

Human food can harm you.

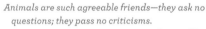

Animals are such agreeable friends—they ask no questions; they pass no criticisms.

—*George Eliot*

Is this squirrel a pest? As one says of a troubled relationship, "it's complicated." We live in an age of blended ecologies, and at least they don't poop on cars, make off with laundry, pester the dog, or yowl all night louder than wet cats. According to the map, this is a non-native species, yet to most kids who see one in the park it's just a squirrel—and hence something to get excited about. Foxes and red-shouldered hawks don't care either. (*Squirrel. It's what's for dinner.*)

At the same time, there's no denying it: in urban and urban-adjacent areas, it outcompetes gray squirrels. Most gardeners hate them and fox squirrels can, at times, be a vector for West Nile virus.

Welcome to the modern world, where even nature study means getting along with neighbors you're not quite sure about.

Yellow-bellied Marmot *Marmota flaviventris*

Don't tell marmots, but they're really just big squirrels. They must think they are prom kings and queens: mink stoled and regal, these ten-pound rodents perch on the top of the tallest boulder around in order to sunbathe while contemplating the universe. Yet one alarm whistle and off they all go, not so much running as shimmying across the ground in a river of golden fur.

This is a mountaintop species at our latitudes; in California don't expect it much below 8,000 feet. It's also a summer-only animal, at least for humans. All summer, marmots eat grass and flowers (and sometimes bird eggs), growing plumper and plumper, then like tiny bears, they hibernate for the winter. If you've grown up east of the Mississippi (or seen the movie *Groundhog Day*), you know the sister species, woodchucks. In all, there are fifteen species of marmots worldwide, ranging from Alaska to Tibet, and our kind, the yellow-bellied marmot, can be found on mountaintops throughout the American West. They do occur in the White Mountains, that austere home to golden eagles and 4,000-year-old bristlecone pines, but they do not live in Mexico or the Andes, so the southern range ends at Mount Whitney.

One way to know you're seeing a marmot and not a regular squirrel (besides size, habitat, and piercing alarm call) is the pale nose. If you can get a good look at the face—binoculars help—it has a pale snout, as if it just got into a bowl of powdered sugar ("Who, me?"). They can become a real nuisance at trailheads: the marmots of Mineral King like to dine on radiator hoses and car wiring. That makes hikers tarp their vehicles, snugging them from the bottom up. That's good sense, because marmots don't just disable vehicles—if you take off in a hurry, they can come along for the ride, stashed inside the engine bay.

The hamster-like pika often shares alpine boulder fields with marmots.

At Mineral King, long-term hikers wrap their cars to keep out marmots.

The woodchuck, or groundhog, is the familiar marmot of the eastern United States.

One other talus-dweller merits notice. The American pika also suns on alpine boulders; it looks like a hamster but is actually related to rabbits. The name is pronounced with a long *i*, as in "pike" and "hike." (Unless you're British, in which case the first syllable rhymes with "peek" and "meek.") The scientific name comes from Mongolian and the common name from Russian, reminding us again that English never met a language it didn't want to snooker out of its life savings. No matter what the name, most people see their first ones along Tioga Pass in Yosemite, but pikas also live in the mining tailings of Bodie, the high-plains ghost town near Bridgeport, and at Eagle Lake, in Mineral King.

I'll tell you how the Sun rose –
A Ribbon at a time –
—Emily Dickinson

Like marmots, pikas harvest summer grass, but they don't hibernate, and they store much of summer's bounty for winter supper. They have small round ears and a twitchy nose, and a grown pika would fit in your two cupped hands. Seeing one—perhaps more so than with any other mountain critter—makes most of us want to plead, "Ah, mom, can I have one? *Pleeeease?*"

California Ground Squirrel *Otospermophilus beecheyi*

With an average of a ten-inch body and seven-inch tail, this is a midsized, out-in-the-daytime squirrel, and if seen well, the dun pelt is spangled with a dazzle of white dots. The eyes are bracketed by pale crescents. It might even be considered handsome if we didn't resent it for spreading bubonic plague and turning fields, parks, and rest stops into a moonscape of burrows and lookout mounds. The range spans from Washington to Baja; California ground squirrels live on Catalina Island (an endemic subspecies) but are not native to the other Channel Islands. Ground squirrels live in colonies, so you won't ever find just one. Watch for them in the campgrounds of Yosemite Valley, along the seashore in Monterey, or in dirt lots everywhere except the most extreme deserts or the highest mountains. They use a sentinel system, so lookouts perch on fence posts and bushes; some scientists suspect they have an extensive grammar and can be quite specific in narrating danger. No matter how we try to parse their syntax, it seems to take only one shout and everybody skedaddles down the nearest hole.

Their caution comes from bitter experience, since every hawk, coyote, and snake out there wants to have squirrel for lunch. Fun fact: ground squirrels chew shed rattlesnake skin and then lick each other, helping to mask their native scent. They will also challenge an intruding snake, scolding and tail-wagging; adults have partial resistance to snake venom, and it benefits the group if they can keep the invader occupied while broadcasting the snake's exact location.

Colonies can include up to a hundred animals, and burrows tunnel and interconnect with all the complexity of a doodled maze on the side of your business notes. The burrows provide refuge for other creatures too, including toads, owls, snakes, salamanders, mole crickets, and stink bugs. To paraphrase John Muir, tug one thread of the universe and you'll find it tied to everything else.

Some books call the main species the Beechey ground squirrel to help separate it from the round-tailed ground squirrel (Anza-Borrego Desert State Park), the Mohave ground squirrel (Desert Tortoise Natural Area, California City), and the Belding's ground squirrel (Mono Lake). All of these look similar and none look anything like the other ground squirrel group, the antelope squirrels. Chipmunk-sized, with white tails, antelope squirrels skitter back and forth in deserts and the Central Valley, their white tails often curled up over their backs. Unlike chipmunks, they never have striped heads. They sprint and stop, as if suddenly puzzled—as one nature buff says, "I love the ground squirrels with white tails over their backs that run like the dickens but then stop and twitch and look like they just forgot where it was they were running to."

Paradise is our native country, and we in this world be as exiles and strangers.
—Richard Greenham

Native Americans used to catch California ground squirrels with snares or by filling the burrows with smoke. They ate the meat and used their pelts for blankets, sewing them with parts of the same animal, since squirrel bones make good awls.

If you want to see this one, you don't need to go much farther than the nearest vacant lot.

Golden-mantled Ground Squirrel

Callospermophilus lateralis

This boldly striped squirrel looks like the chipmunks that follow in the next few pages but is larger and always has a plain (not striped) face; and unlike chipmunks, it mostly stays on the ground rather than dashing up the trunks of trees.

Found in most Sierra and northern forests, golden-mantled ground squirrels are active from late spring to early fall, fossicking for tubers, sniffing out underground fungi, nipping flowers buds in the bud, and feasting on pine seeds, acorns, grasshoppers, bird eggs, lizards, and even carrion. They prefer a mixed or open forest, especially woodland with rock piles or fallen timber. That means we should expect it among the trees, not in the middle of wet meadows. Food, food, food, and more food is what's on its mind, as it accumulates fat to carry it through hibernation. Cheek pouches bulge with each successful foray, and by late summer it has added 80 percent to its body weight.

What cues tell it that autumn has arrived and that it's time to stop eating and start hibernating? Perhaps it waits for the smell of pumpkin spice latte to drift up from the lowlands, but if that's absent then it can rely on the combination of shorter days, colder nights, and a general decrease in the food supply. During winter, activity varies by sex: one study discovered that adult males entered hibernation later, emerged earlier, spent less time in torpor, and had fewer sequential days in deep sleep than either females or juveniles. (Females may need to conserve energy in order to give birth, which happens before emergence.) In Alaska, arctic ground squirrels can survive body temperatures dropping below freezing. If we understood the physics of hibernation better, then all those sci-fi movies about sleeping our way to Jupiter could be an inch closer to reality.

> The discovery of spring each year, after the winter's hibernation, is like a rediscovery of the universe.
>
> —Louis Halle

It's hard to measure IQ precisely, but this is one animal that understands the true purpose of national park vista points. Animals can't read the *Do Not Feed the Squirrels* signs in national parks and apparently neither can many visitors, since obese and semi-tame squirrels can be found begging for food in campgrounds, by snack bars, at pullouts, and any place children comingle with potato chips.

Chipmunks Neotamias spp

"I don't paint things," Matisse reportedly said. "I only paint the differences between things." With chipmunks he would have had his hands full because we have thirteen species, and their differences can be quite subtle. Range maps help, as does noting altitude and the pattern of dark-light-dark on the stripes, but the fact is, even for experienced naturalists, most chipmunks look pretty much alike, and many have overlapping ranges. In museums, one way to confirm ID is by checking the baculum or penis bone, since shape varies by species. It must have been somebody's Ph.D. dissertation to gather that data, and just be glad it was not yours.

What is a chipmunk? A chipmunk is a squirrel on bennies, a tree-dashing busybody who wants to know what's in your lunch bag or, wait, no—needs to go find out what those redwood trees are doing, *right now*. If you ever go to Siberia there's a chipmunk species there, but as a group chipmunks mostly fill out the top half of the North American map; there are no chipmunks south of Mexico. Chipmunks are usually smaller than squirrels, though like them they have the same appetite for nuts and seeds, buds and shoots, mushrooms and bird eggs. In California, most species stick to pines, but some extend down into the oaks and even desert chaparral and sagebrush.

> *I am a great fan of the universe, which I take literally: as one. All of it interests me, and it interests me in detail.*
> —*Diane Ackerman*

Very few animals resemble chipmunks, and none overlap completely. The antelope squirrel is nearly the same size and also has stripes, but it has a white tail and lives in deserts and valleys. The golden-mantled ground squirrel shares a love of forests and has a striped back, but it is always bigger and has a yellow face. Douglas squirrels (sometimes called chickarees) are nearly small enough to match, and also live in Yosemite and Tahoe, but they are dark red-brown with a pale eye-ring. Basically, if it's small and striped and way too manic, it's a chipmunk.

In winter a chipmunk hibernates, though it is less like suspended animation and more like taking very long naps. Every few days they wake up, eat something, have a wee, and then go

Antelope squirrels look like chipmunks but are never found in forests. This one snacks on birdseed on a wall in the desert town of Trona.

Like chipmunks, Antelope squirrels have striped sides; unlike chipmunks, they have white tails.

At left, a least chipmunk eats something it shouldn't in Bodie. Right, Uinta chipmunk, White Mountains.

back to sleep. Yet when they're conked out, they're *really* out, and body temp drops low, lower, lowest, and their hearts barely beat. Warm winters disrupt this pattern, causing them to use up their food reserves or emerge too soon, increasing the risk of running into a hawk or weasel. How climate change may alter populations cannot yet be predicted.

Alvin and the Chipmunks aside, the common name does replicate the vocal range, and scientists trying to categorize their bright, sharp calls use terms like "chip," "chuck," and "trill." Hearing it for the first time you might think it is an angry sparrow scolding a recalcitrant cat, or maybe somebody whose chirping remote unlocks a somewhat distant, very annoying car. (Others claim it sounds like a stuck cork being worked out of a tight bottle.)

Chipmunks do make an appearance in art. There is John James Audubon of course, and Canadian wildlife artist Robert Bateman paints chipmunks with the same love and royal presence he gives his lions and tigers. In the American Museum of Natural History in New York there is a diorama of an okapi deep in the Congo. In the painted background, hiding in plain sight, there is a whimsical chipmunk on the forest floor.

It is a sly joke, since chipmunks don't live in Africa.

American Beaver and Muskrat

Castor canadensis and *Ondatra zibethicus*

How to build a beaver: it's aquatic, so we need webbed feet, and a tail that helps steer, paddle, and sound the alarm. How about built-in goggles—be sure to install nictitating membranes over the eyes. Valves on ears and nose, to keep out water. To extend that idea, we need a tongue that can close off the throat, so you can gnaw willow trunks under the water and not choke. Specialized microbiota in the gut to digest stems. It's cold, especially in winter, so large body size reduces the volume-to-surface ratio. Follow that up with a heat exchange system so that blood leaving the warm core and headed out to the cold feet and tail transfers its warmth to the blood passing back in. And last, we need a really good pelt: a dense layer of insulating inner fur protected by long, waterproof guard hairs.

Oops—it was that last item that was almost the end of beavers in America. There are two species of beavers in the world, American and European, and both can be used to make hats. After you have killed either kind, skin it, shave the underhair, beat those hairs and cook them and turn them into felt, and then that felt can be steamed and turned into a shiny, waterproof, fashionable hat. The mercury needed for processing will make hatters mad and the fur trade will depopulate the rivers of the American West, but those top hats, oh, how nice they will look.

At right: Beavers in the desert?
Yes, they live along the Colorado River.

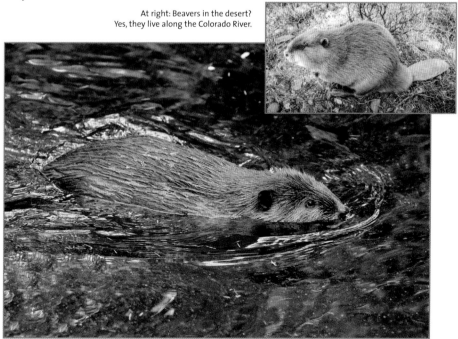

The trappers got most but not all American beavers, and they can still be found in the San Joaquin and Sacramento River systems, along the Colorado River, and in the Northern California mountains. Historically they were also present in all of the coastal creeks and rivers, from Del Norte County to Bodega Bay to Santa Monica to San Diego. We want them back: beavers and their engineering works help recharge groundwater, prevent soil erosion, and enhance willow forests that in turn are used by warblers and vireos.

Besides the beaver—and excluding escapee capybaras, an Amazon species that is the largest rodent in the world—we have another wetland animal to remember in California. A muskrat is basically the same as a beaver, just smaller and with a slimmer tail that isn't flat like a beaver's. The name comes from the general shape (rather ratlike) and the scent glands that help mark territory. Native to North America but introduced to California, they too can make mounds and lodges but also burrow dens into the banks, and the burrows may at times weaken levees in the Sacramento Delta. Often nocturnal, muskrats eat cattails and aquatic vegetation (and sometimes crayfish).

Do unto those downstream as you would have those upstream do unto you.
—Wendell Berry

As for what to do with the rest of the beaver after you have made your hat, according to church law, a beaver is really a kind of fish. If you're hungry, that's good news, since it means you can eat it any day of the week—even on a Friday and even during Lent.

Above, even if you don't spot any beavers at Taylor Creek Marsh in Lake Tahoe, the site's beauty makes up for it.
Left, a muskrat is smaller than a beaver and has a slim, round tail.

Pocket Gophers *Thomomys* spp

It's not just an old joke: once gophers get going, their fan-shaped dirt piles really *do* fill up the lawn, and some meadows are 20 percent gopher mounds. Don't yell at them though or wish they would all migrate away like Alaska-bound lemmings. Instead, be glad they're here (more on that in a moment) and pause to admire their fossorial success. Gophers use beaver-proud incisors to mow grass and shear roots, while at the same time managing to store bulging wads of food in their cheek pouches, breathing without choking on dirt, staying alert for hawks and foxes, and orienting themselves inside a spatial ecology one million times larger, brighter, stranger, and riskier than the all-dark, body-sized tunnels where they spend the majority of their year. When the mama gopher says to the family, "All right, children, time to go out and forage for shoots and leaves," who could blame them for a chorus of "Aww mom, do we gotta?"

Five to eight inches long, pocket gophers take the "pocket" part of their name because of their cheek pouches. They harvest food above and below ground, and yes, as in the cartoons, they will take out a whole row of carrots. Their front teeth are long, curved, and perpetually growing; pocket gophers also have long, sharp

A gopher's-eye view of Yosemite.

Above, left and right: Botta's pocket gopher.

claws that would probably cause nightmares if anybody ever made gophers the stars of horror films. The most common of our five species is the Botta's pocket gopher, named for Paolo Emilio Botta, an Italian doctor serving on a French ship that visited California in 1827. We'll try not to envy his glimpse of heaven: the skies full of condors, the rivers full of salmon and grizzly bears, and the hillsides blazing orange with poppies. (He also gave his name to a bat in Yemen and a gerbil in Somalia, so a tip of the hat to somebody who sure knew how to get around.)

Reality is a slippery concept, because it is not separate from us. Reality is in our minds.
—David Hockney

They are usually solitary, other than in the breeding season; one gopher maintains a solo complex of tunnels. Besides being their homes, these holes allow deep penetration of water during rainstorms, preventing erosion and facilitating water recharge. Gopher burrows use a radius of space efficiently, zigzagging out and back like a cross between a multibranched snowflake and a scribble of loosely coiled yarn. Inside the tunnel are separate chambers for eating, sleeping, and defecating; the total complex may be more than fifty yards long. Like a hobbit hole, a gopher mound has a front door, though theirs is just a solid plug of dirt. Often it matches the displaced soil so well you can't tell where mound stops and burrow entrance begins.

Moles are much harder to see above ground and don't have the exposed teeth of a gopher. Their mounds are usually volcano-shaped rather than uneven or fan-shaped, and moles are less likely to be found in packed or stony ground.

Often "hiding in plain sight," pocket gophers like city parks, interstate rest stops, college campuses, pastures, meadows, and (alas) your newly seeded garden.

Top right: Mountain pocket gopher mound.
Middle right: Townsend's mole mound.
Middle left: Botta's pocket gopher mound (note door plug).
Bottom: Botta's pocket gopher inches out cautiously.

Kangaroo Rats *Dipodomys* spp

We first met these in the introduction: kangaroo rats are the long-tailed ricochets of tan fur seen on desert roads at night. Bigger than mice and smaller than squirrels, all kangaroo rats are sandy brown on top and white underneath; many biologists affectionately call them k-rats. On average, the tufted tails are even longer than their bodies, yet the entire combination only weighs a few ounces.

There are thirteen species in California, and besides thriving in the low and high deserts, they also inhabit coastal chaparral and interior grasslands like the Carrizo Plain (where you can see three kinds in one night). They live in burrows and forage on open ground, harvesting seeds that they store in bulging cheek pouches. If they're alarmed, powerfully sprung legs shoot them ahead like bottle rockets, the entire burst of energy counterbalanced by a lively tail that streams behind or, when they pause, may ribbon beside them on the ground in an elegant S.

Like any responsible Californian, kangaroo rats know how to conserve water, extracting moisture from their food and concentrating urine so they only pee out a few drops. A nocturnal lifestyle lets them snooze through the heat of the day and a cozy burrow means their own breath can raise the humidity, which they

Merriam's kangaroo rat.

Jawbone Canyon in the Mojave Desert is home to
kangaroo rats by night and LeConte's thrashers by day.

One way to identify kangaroo rats is to count their toes.

breathe back in. In laboratory tests, if offered water of course they will drink it, but on summer nights in the desert, they have a lifestyle that can do without.

They are eaten by more or less anything with sharp teeth or talons, so to warn other k-rats of a predator, the one who spots danger first drums babaloo very rapidly with its large hind feet. Overall, they prefer darker nights to those of a full moon, and cloud cover to open sky, but those trends vary depending on food sources and the state of cover. They also are willing to confront snakes, getting very close and then jumping straight up, or else turning around and kicking up a hailstorm of grit onto the snake's head. (And it's not like the snake can put up its hands to cover its eyes.) One study suggests that the jumping displays remind the snake how easily it can get away, thus warning them not to waste their time even trying. Since a kangaroo rat can leap eight feet, this is not an empty boast.

If you have not encountered kangaroo rats yet in Death Valley or Joshua Tree, you may have seen one on a wanted poster, since there are hopes that some

The more we exile ourselves from nature, the more we crave its miracle waters.
—Diane Ackerman

could still exist around Mount Diablo not far from San Francisco. Another place they can be absurdly common is Lava Beds National Monument, or in Southern California, in the foothill areas of the Antelope Valley. Patience has its rewards: if you see a kangaroo rat, approaching slowly with a flashlight often lets you get quite close. Frank Stephens, an early biologist who now has a species of kangaroo rat named for him, used to sit so quietly at his campsites that k-rats would scamper right across his feet.

Deer Mice *Peromyscus* spp

Flash and blink: it may not be the easiest little animal to see, yet the deer mouse is found just about everywhere in California, from alpine meadows to the Colorado River. In the singular, "deer mouse" refers to the North American deer mouse, or one can speak of "deer mice" plural, a group of seven that includes the canyon mouse, cactus mouse, brush mouse, and piñon mouse.

Though they sometimes come out during the day, deer mice are mostly nocturnal; they are also active year-round. Spot it as it pokes a curious head out of a cabin's woodpile, or perhaps you'll see it in headlights as it scoots across a rural road. In the photo at right, a deer mouse on the Carrizo Plain had fallen in love with my truck tires. It would hide in the rims and then dart out to explore the campsite, then quickly retreat once a flashlight caught up with it. After you learn to watch for them, you'll see them more and more often. While living at Walden Pond, Henry David Thoreau had a pet deer mouse—as did George Armstrong Custer when he was on campaign in the Dakota Territory.

Deer mice eat seeds but also insects, fungus, acorns, plant leaves—whatever they can get. They are snoutier than a house mouse (see page 43); with bigger ears; tan-above, white-below countershading (unlike a house mouse's plain gray); and an ability to thrive undetected by most of us big folk. The different deer mice species can overlap, with up to four kinds being found in the same area. Habitat and color differences help split them apart, so that canyon mouse likes cliffs and talus slopes, and the cactus mouse, a drabber tan, is the low desert kind, common,

Star Wars Canyon in Death Valley is a good place to see canyon mice and jets such as this EA-18G Growler.

Top: This woodrat nest in a juniper was five feet across.

Middle left: A North American deer mouse makes a sortie from the author's truck.

Right: Large eyes and even larger ears reveal adaptations necessary for a nocturnal lifestyle.

Left: North American deer mouse. Right: The brush mouse often investigates cabins.

for example, in the lower elevations of Joshua Tree National Park. It concentrates urine and feces and can live without ever drinking water.

We pause here to ask a basic question: Do mice even matter? In nature, what do they *do*? One answer is they don't need to do anything, if we agree that all life has an equal right to exist and the great chain of being contains infinite links. But another perspective comes from the biologist who answered without hesitation, "What do they do? Deer mice convert grass and seeds into themselves, which is to say, into bite-sized bundles of protein, thus sustaining owls, snakes, kestrels, weasels, bobcats, and everything in between." They may also have a small role to play in soil aeration and plant regeneration (via seed caches), but it could be true: the deer mouse's greatest fans may be the many other pouncers and grabbers that require a stable and abundant prey base so in turn they can go forth and multiply.

Since it's found in so many habitats, deer mice win the everywhere-at-once-and-twice-on-Sundays award. In them we see how the basic rodent template makes such a successful body plan. It can be scaled up, giving us the woodrat series. They're the

Fork my tongue, Lord. There is a sorrow on the air
I taste but cannot name. I want to open
my mouth and know the exact
flavor of what's to come, I want to open
my mouth and sound a language
that calls all language home.

—Nickole Brown

ones also called pack rats whose stick nests grow to be eight feet around and become compressed into fossilized strata, sometimes going back thousands of years. (You can see deer mice and woodrats in the same field, and even the same nest, but woodrats are always bigger.) Going the other direction, you can shrink the template down, so that we have the pocket mice, most of which look like the *Honey, I Shrunk the Kids* version of deer mice, so small they barely weigh a quarter of an ounce (which is less than a couple of pennies).

The "deer" in deer mice refers to the color, which matches the two-tone paint job of the East Coast's white-tailed deer.

House Mouse *Mus musculus*

Few organisms have hitched their wagon to our star with as much success as the house mouse. It has now spread to more places in the world than Diet Coke, McDonald's, and Amazon combined. Only the cold virus can claim better market penetration. Do the tribal elders remind the little mice about the time—so long ago, yet still remembered—when they were all just wet little nothings, eking out a miserable living in northern India? But then the god of agriculture picked them (them!) as the Chosen Ones, and invented grain silos, invented cities, invented attics and insulated walls and boxes of Cheerios, and their true destiny was revealed.

Unlike deer mice (tan above, pale below) the house mouse is gray or dark brown and naked-tailed and human-centric, so ID features are fairly obvious. My favorite place to study them is the London Underground, though I once had one that lived inside my kitchen stove in Papua New Guinea, and it adroitly managed to avoid the oven burners, day after day. "Small as a mouse" is not inaccurate: six of them weigh less than a paper cup of house blend. Even the root word in Proto-Indo-European is small—basically a variation on "mus." Few of us would begrudge them a few grams of daily bread, but the problem is the mess—droppings and urine in the food, wires chewed up, first editions shredded—and of course the inevitable and Malthusian population rise. One mouse becomes one hundred mice very quickly.

White lab mice are this same species, as are the pet store mice people feed to snakes; neither should be released in nature. Fancy mice (as pet varieties are called) come in such forms as banded, satin, champagne, blue tan, and lilac—names so attractive they would make nice wedding presents. (If bikers raised mice, would their strains be called road rash and hangover?)

The house mouse is one of the most ur-species in this book, something that all cultures discuss and all children can name from an early age, perhaps even before learning cow, pig, goat, or duck. We are trained to dislike them and to associate their presence with poverty or slovenly house-keeping, but perhaps we should acknowledge the reality of their endurance. The house mouse is one kick-ass survivor, and it is not a sign of dirt or lassitude—it can be found in plenty of highfalutin places too. On some islands near New Zealand they are an ecological menace, but on average, because they like towns more than nature, their impact on other species is no better or worse than our own.

A man taught art at a university. When he came home after work his daughter asked him what he did that day. He said, "I taught people how to draw." And she said, "People forget how to draw?"

—Mary Ruefle

All praise the common house mouse—and a toast to our next 5,000 years.

Roof Rat and Norway Rat

Rattus rattus and *Rattus norvegicus*

We have two non-native rats. The roof rat—aka black rat, house rat, ship rat—is the smaller, longer-tailed one; it nests in attics or trees (including the untrimmed "beards" of palm trees). It occurs worldwide but in North America lives in a crescent from Washington to California and along the snowbird belt to Florida. Infected fleas hosted by this species caused the Black Death in Europe in the fourteenth century.

The burrow-nesting Norway rat (brown rat, wharf rat, sewer rat) is a bit larger and on average a bit more successful—it likes cities too, but is even more global, spreading across inland North America. In general, it outcompetes roof rats along the immediate coast or in colder areas.

Both are common (even abundant) yet rarely seen—for one thing we are usually in cars or trains, and for another, rats represent another invisible California population surviving in the shadows. When it comes to rats in public, New York City easily beats California for the quantity and bravura of its daylight rats, with one Upper West Side park being called "the Burning Man of rats."

Norway rats are browner than roof rats (which often are all-black), but there's so much variation, color alone doesn't clinch identification. Instead, look at the tail: the roof rat's tail is longer than the head and body combined. In Norway rats the tail is the same length or shorter than the

> *The world reveals itself to those who travel on foot.*
>
> —Werner Herzog

Above and left: Roof rat *Rattus rattus*.

Roof rat *Rattus rattus.*

Above and right: Norway rat *Rattus norvegicus.*

body. All rats eat everything and anything, breed readily, swim well, climb trees, cliffs, and power lines, and easily wiggle through surprisingly small pipes and grates. They've been in California at least since the 1850s (and probably for seventy-five years before that). Norway rats—native originally to China, by the way, not Scandinavia—are the same as white lab rats. California agriculture gladly would see them all locked up for lethal injection, since Norway rats take rice and other grain directly from the field, and then they come back for seconds once the harvest is siloed up for storage.

From numerical and cultural perspectives, as it spread through Western Europe, the Black Death was apocalyptic, and yet some of its results we might point to with approval. These include the rising value and hence mobility of labor—suddenly peasants were a desired commodity—or the fact that wolves were able to expand their populations into new, de facto wilderness areas. Bubonic plague today seems to be a less virulent strain, plus for many residents of Northern European ancestry, by definition we're partially immune. If our genetic ancestors had not had a high tolerance for rats, fleas, plagues, and fevers, none of us would have made it as far as we have today.

North American Porcupine *Erethizon dorsatum*

All hail the quill pig (to celebrate one of its folk names). Porcupines are large, solitary, plant-grazing, tree-bark-gnawing rodents; ours is the northernmost member of a diverse South American family. As fabulous as the local one is, in the jungle some are even better: they are gold and black and have prehensile tails. (Porcupines are also found in the Old World; a North African species was introduced into Italy by the Romans.) In California the porcupine's range includes mountains and river valleys in the northern half of the state (including the peaks of Death Valley National Park), but they are not found in Angeles Crest, San Diego, or the Channel Islands.

The body almost seems like a prank or hoax—what do you get when you cross a skunk with a cactus?—yet this is one stout little tank, with 30,000 quills and a body that weighs up to 25 pounds. Porcupines rustle or even sort of clack when they walk, and if you find a shed quill on the ground it is strangely light and yet fiercely sharp—imagine a knitting needle that weighs less than a soda straw yet tapers to a point sharper than a tranquilizer dart.

Left alone, porcupines wander through the forest or climb trees or trundle along the edges of meadows. All that changes if threatened: the black-and-white spines razorback into full defense mode and the entire animal suddenly looks larger and meaner. The teeth chatter menacingly and a stinky smell leaks out. Even though the quills are made from keratin—the same as fingernails and horse hooves—they detach easily and are finely barbed, so once in they not only stay in, but over time, they work in even deeper. Luckily for us this is all just defensive weaponry: a rampaging porcupine can't gallop up and shoot quills *bing bing bing* into your dog's nose—any quills that end up there are entirely the dog's own fault.

Some mountain lions know how to flip a porcupine over to get at its relatively unprotected belly, and you'll come across roadside porcupines that have been killed by cars; but mostly they are a robust and successful beast, enviable and iconic. How do you know if they're around? The scat looks like chubby black jellybeans, and in the snow, porcupine tracks include the side-to-side drag marks left by its whisk broom tail.

Reported vocalizations include moans, grunts, coughs, wails, whines, shrieks, and tooth clicking. Males urinate on the females during courtship, adding a new layer of meaning to the old joke, "How do porcupines make love?" (Answer: "Carefully.")

Because you have seen something doesn't mean you can explain it.

— Barry Lopez

The more we learn about them, the stranger and more enigmatic porcupines become.

Feral Pig *Sus scrofa*

Most animals move through the landscape with a fairly light touch. Deer browse and antelope graze, but then we have feral pigs. Sometimes called razorbacks, feral swine resemble turbocharged rototillers—ransacking woods, churning springs into wallows, and leaving topsoil peeled back like the trenches of a looted archaeological dig.

History combines with genetics to cause this. By the early 1800s, California's domesticated pigs—descended from and still related to wild boars—had begun to escape and become feral. These were often semi-free-ranging to begin with, managed by a swineherd and feeding on acorn mast and other forest products. In addition to those pigs, hunters in the 1920s released European wild boars for sport, but that stock had a backwash of domestic pig genetics sloshing around in it too, so in California today a pig is a boar is a boar is a pig except when it is a pig-boar, aka the real monsters with folk names like Hogzilla. (And yes, North America does also have one native pig, the collared peccary or javelina, but it's only present in California in zoos.)

Black, red, spotted, or in between, California's 70,000 feral pigs come in as many colors as they do habitats, including woodland, grassland, canebrakes, riverbeds, and chaparral. They can weigh up to eight hundred pounds (though two hundred is more usual), and both females and males have five-inch tusks. A herd is called a sounder and a sounder of pigs will gobble up all the bird eggs, amphibians, and tender shoots it comes across. Feral pigs undercut roads and trample crops. "Feral swine are an ecological train wreck," says Craig Hicks, a biologist with the US Department of Agriculture's Wildlife Services. One study suggests that "wild pigs are perhaps the most prolific large mammal on Earth." Every manager of natural resources in California agrees that feral pigs need to go.

The truth does not change according to our ability to stomach it.
—Flannery O'Connor

Ah yes, but go where? To pig heaven? (The pigs would say they've already arrived there.) Large-scale trapping is impractical, as is pig-by-pig contraception. One option—one of the few control methods that works at all—is hunting. That, though, raises the same ethical questions as culling mustangs or trapping house mice: whose world is it, and what do we do if our basic "right to life" instincts make us prefer not to harm other beings? Yet hunting makes sense if the health of ecosystems matters most. Perhaps we can imagine a future day when the NRA, Earth First!, and the Sierra Club agree to form a pig-management coalition. As with the campaign to eradicate the Burmese python in the Everglades, prizes can be given out for the largest tusks, the heaviest animals, and the best recipes for sharing the harvest.

Pass the *chicharrón*.

Pronghorn *Antilocapra americana*

Fast, faster, fastest: we have not had wild cheetahs in California since the Ice Age, but if they ever come back, the pronghorn are ready. They are the only native animal in North America that can be chased by a full-grown cheetah and still cross the finish line first.

The pronghorn is a white-sided, white-throated, white-rumped relative of the deer; the slim black horns stick straight up about as high as the length of the head. Seen from the front, the horns hook down at the top, like two hands signing a heart. Both males and females have antlers, which are shed and regrown annually. (See "Mule Deer," page 67 for more on antlers versus horns.)

How fast do they go? Pick any speed between forty and seventy miles an hour and some website somewhere will list it. Edging up toward sixty seems reasonable. (Faster than humans anyway.) Even when they are standing still, identification is easy. Any big brown pony with a downward curling rack is a bighorn sheep, while mule deer are darker than pronghorn (never so blond)—plus a male deer's set of antlers reaches higher and branches with more tines. An elk will always be the biggest brown deer in the forest that is not a stray cow. That just leaves the pronghorn, which, despite also being called the pronghorn antelope, is not a true antelope but looks close enough to those for the name to work. We

hear that echo in the famous song "Home on the Range," which praises a place "where the deer and the antelope play."

Once common throughout the Central Valley, the high deserts, and coastal plains, pronghorn remain more Californian than we might think. Native Americans used to hunt them, and antelope place names fill the map, including variations on "*berrendo*," which is what Spanish settlers called them. When the first Northern European settlers in San Diego tried to grow crops, antelope came at night and ate them all up. Soon they became even more rare. Declines happened for the usual reasons—indiscriminate hunting, not enough grass, not enough water, too many feral dogs, too many fences. Deer

From what we cannot hold, the stars are made.
—W. S. Merwin

go over (or through) a fence, but pronghorn jump poorly and try to go under. In Southern California wild pronghorn lasted at least until 1941 (Chuckwalla Mountains, Riverside County). Urban legend places them in L.A.'s Antelope Valley that late as well, though that area is also the home of the Flat Earth Society and a fair number of UFO sightings, so some local claims may be suspect.

Today herds can be looked for across the northeast section of the state—one nickname for the Great Basin being the Big Empty, which usually means there's lots of room for wildlife. A few were released on Tejon Ranch property near Gorman but with mixed results. Closer to the coast (just two hours from Santa

Barbara), pronghorn can be seen in the grasslands of Carrizo Plain National Monument, where a herd was reintroduced in the 1980s—a good place also for badgers, kit foxes, kangaroo rats, and wide-open vistas.

If you've not seen one yet, you might wonder if it's worth the trouble. Answer: yes with an extra helping of yes. There's a grace and beauty to pronghorn that no native California animal can match. Bernd Heinrich is best known for his work with ravens, but he has insights into other kinds of wildlife as well. As he says—getting the poetics of indeterminacy exactly right—a pronghorn "seems ambiguous, hovering as it does in between the real that you can touch and the humanly unattainable."

Some animals take us past ourselves, past our imaginations, and this is one of them.

Bighorn Sheep *Ovis canadensis*

If you've been to Anza-Borrego, the desert park east of San Diego, the name combines two kinds of history. Juan Bautista de Anza was a Basque-Spanish explorer, while "*borrego*" is the Spanish word for bighorn sheep. That park can be a good place to see them, but it's mostly about luck: the Mount Baldy side of Angeles Crest is possible too, or Mount San Jacinto as it rises past you on the Palm Springs tram, or maybe the Eastern Sierra coming out of Tioga Pass, or just close your eyes and dream, since lots of wildlife can be out there even if we may not see it in person as often as we like. That doesn't mean that it's not there and not still keeping our spirits lifted just a scosh higher.

Brown with a white rump, the bighorn is deer sized but stockier. Bachelor herds and groups of females, called ewes, often stay separate except during breeding. Both sexes have horns, which start alert and upright and begin to sweep downward with age. During the rut, head-butting males bash into each other with resounding crashes, protected from concussions by

I don't know how to start, but perhaps that's no matter. I am only 35 years old, and the land is more than a billion; how can I be expected to know what to say beyond "Please" and "Thank you" and "Ma'am"?
—*Rick Bass*

strong bones and internal air-sac shock absorbers. Like tree rings, the horns indicate age: the older the sheep, the larger the horn and the more spiraled its curl.

Rock climbers wish they had the sure-footedness of this cliff inhabitant; to out-climb the things that want to eat you (mountain lions, for example) means that "sheer" and "inaccessible" go into your Zillow searches first. There is some altitudinal migration; in the Sierra and Angeles Crest, snow levels push herds lower, or in summer, the location of water matters a lot.

According to one nineteenth-century source, "the old stories of bighorn jumping over cliffs and alighting on their horns are untrue." What more can we say? You read it here first.

North American Elk *Cervus canadensis*

When Manifest Destiny came west in 1846, a confederation of Northern European settlers tried to wrestle Alta California from the Mexican government. This rebel alliance needed a flag, and, famously, made a version of what we have now: red star, the words "California Republic," and a strolling grizzly bear. (Originally the bear was standing up.)

It didn't have to be a bear, of course—why not an elk? After all, compared to a grizzly, our two kinds of native elk (the Roosevelt, in the coastal redwoods, and the tule elk, everywhere else) are majestic survivors. Tall and broad shouldered, these robust mega-deer were originally found throughout the state, and in the case of the tule elk, numbered a half million or more. Their name references tules (pronounced "toolies"): the reeds and cattails in the wetlands that once ran from the Grapevine up through Sacramento and all the way to Redding. Unlike the grizzly bear, both elk subspecies survive today; among other places, look for tule elk at Point Reyes National Seashore and in the Owens Valley and up in the far northeast, and expect Roosevelt elk in the state and national parks in the coastal rain belt.

> *To appreciate grass, you must lie down in grass.*
>
> —Louise Erdrich

Tule elk.

All elk are brown with a blond butt; only males grow antlers. The group name is gang, while a young male is a spike. Legs and neck are often darker brown than the tan body; you can always tell an elk from a mule deer by body mass and this two-tone pelage. Starting in spring, the bull elk grow antlers, and they would agree, "the bigger, the better." Antlers start as layers of cartilage covered by blood-rich skin; this later hardens to pure bone as the velvet covering peels off. A full set of antlers weighs up to forty pounds and indicates health, age, and robust genes. Bugling and head-bashing, bulls compete for control of a herd of cows and calves. We lack good descriptive words for bugling; some sources use phrases like *a bellow that rises to a squeal and ends with a grunt*. Ah yes, music to a lady elk's ears.

Tule elk.

California's tule and Roosevelt elk are each related to the Rocky Mountain elk that lives in Yellowstone, and all elk were once thought to be the same as the red deer in Europe and Asia. That *ménage à trois* has been split into separate North American, Asian, and European species. Meanwhile American elk have been introduced to New Zealand and red deer to North America.

To mix it up even more, the Irish elk is none of these; it is an extinct Ice Age species that looked like the cross between a giant moose and a giraffe. Then in Europe there is yet another animal called an elk, which in American English we would call a moose. To straighten all this out, some people suggest using "wapiti" (from a Shawnee word) to label North American kinds, but that option has not yet caught on, especially not in California.

Roosevelt elk.

Roosevelt elk.

Tule elk.

When camera maker Canon helped fund the reestablishment of the elk herd at Point Reyes, these large, photogenic, and roadside-browsing animals instantly became a hit with tourists. As we consider so many confusing terms and blurred taxonomy, it seems that the cosponsor of elk rehabilitation should have been Merriam-Webster.

Mule Deer *Odocoileus hemionus*

Named for their large oval ears, mule deer are robust and ubiquitous. You expect them in Yosemite, yet at Morro Bay you'll find their tracks crisscrossing saltwater beaches, while in the high deserts deer follow the brush out of the mountains into Joshua Tree National Park. Some books make a distinction between Sierra mule deer and the coastal variety called black-tailed deer, but both subspecies have black-tipped tails and look more or less the same. North America's other main deer, the white-tailed deer, does not occur in California; it has a white hand-kerchief tail and a different antler pattern. Mule deer antlers fork as they grow, like twigs from a branch from a main branch; white-tailed antlers stick up from a single main beam, like irrigation canals leaving a river.

Hide, hooves, meat, fat: all parts were once used by Native Americans, who used to capture deer using snares and pitfall traps, or in communal drives. Mountain lions rely on mule deer as a main food item; though for such a keystone

species, deer remain understudied: for example, what role do they play in maintaining (or altering) the vegetation of native botanical complexes? We can discover deer just by looking up more often—you might even see them beside I-5 in Gorman on your way into L.A. for Thanksgiving, or maybe browsing within sight of the Golden Gate Bridge. If that strategy doesn't work, try checking the berms of mountain roads: the astounding quantity of car-struck deer carcasses reveals how common they are—and also how badly we drive.

Above: Mule deer are even found in Mojave National Preserve.

As with moose and elk (and unlike bighorn sheep and pronghorn), only males grow antlers, which drop off in late winter after the rut. When first growing, the antlers have a covering of skin and blood vessels, the "velvet" that later dries up and peels off. Antlers are not the same as horns: antlers grow anew each year while horns are permanent. Structure differs too, since antlers are all bone while horns are layers of keratin accumulating over a bone core. In the phosphorous cycle of forest ecology, antlers do more than just help boy deer impress girl deer. Since antlers are chockablock with calcium, shed antlers don't last long on the forest floor. When they find them, rodents like voles and chipmunks gnaw away, happy for a source of minerals.

When the canneries were active in Monterey, sardine boats sported mule deer antlers on the crow's nests. They supposedly brought good luck—at least to the boats if not to the deer.

Deer cannot see red or orange, a biologist writes, but apparently can see blue much better than we can. Who can even imagine what that would mean, for blue to be—well, more?
—Mark Doty

Mustang and Feral Burro

Equus caballus and *Equus africanus*

From cigarettes ads to *Brokeback Mountain*, cowboys epitomize the lonely courage of American horizons. It's a two-part equation, since without his horse a cowboy is nothing but a bowlegged farmer. Stetson and six-shooter optional, but the horse is essential.

Equines (zebras, horses, and donkeys) first evolved 4 million years ago. The horse lasted in North America until the end of the Ice Age, disappearing either because of changing climate or hunting pressure by newly arriving humans (or both). Horses didn't return until the 1500s, when Native Americans liberated the conquistadors' Iberian mounts. The ones that got away returned to ancestral landscapes, and they've been present in the West ever since.

Horses in the wild form small groups called bands, sometimes coalescing into something large enough to be called a herd. Along shared pathways (such as trails to water holes) horses—especially stallions—scent-mark like dogs, leaving dung and urine to claim territory and announce status. A dominant stallion frets and charges, guarding his harem of mares and the foals of both sexes. The leftover males form bachelor herds, watching for a chance to challenge the big guy; deposed stallions may end up exiled as a herd of one.

As is often true elsewhere, boys are less in charge than they may think; the boss mare usually decides when the band will head out to find water, stick around because the grazing is good, or spend the night here and not there. Mares also follow their hearts—according to DNA studies, up to a third of the foals in a given herd can have out-of-band fathers.

Related to tapirs and rhinos, horses have prehensile lips and can adroitly graze the stubble of even the stoniest steppe. Horses can snort, whinny, nicker, and neigh—or do several at once: *Willll-burrrr*. Made from the same stuff as fingernails, a horse hoof is basically a hard, extended, single toe. Other fun facts? Horses adore

Mustang Crossing sign near Death Valley.

acorns but too many can kill them; they can also develop a powerful hankering for pomegranates, apples, carrots, watermelon, and (at least in India), bananas. Largest eye of any land animal. The word "stale" used to refer to horse urine, not old bread. For the Scrabble players among us, mustangs in Australia are called brumbies.

Eaten by nothing other than the occasional mountain lion, horses in most of their range have multiplied past what the habitat can sustain. Do we herd and cull, awarding priority at water holes to natives like bighorn sheep, or do we call horses legacy animals and try to find a way to let them fit in? The Bureau of Land Management estimates that herds double in size every five years.

Feral burros mirror this trend. Native originally to Africa and domesticated 5,000 years ago, they too came here with the conquistadors and from the 1860s onwards have populated remote parts of the American

I believe there is a space within the human heart reserved especially for a relationship with the horse.

—Bonnie L. Hendricks

Mares and foals graze under big skies.

Wild Horse Roundup, 1923.

West. After a lot of fuss and bother they were eradicated from Death Valley National Park, which built a thirty-four-mile fence. Walls rarely work; in the park they number in the thousands again. Are burros non-native pests or colorful reminders of our prospector heritage? Either way, we have a lot of them, and driving late at night in Big Bear or Death Valley one needs to be careful not to hit one.

The BLM is working on methods of contraception but also rounds up excess animals. In pens across the West, there are thousands of surplus horses and donkeys waiting for adoption. According to tradition, Nietzsche's last act was to embrace a horse.

Right: A modern burro, the ultimate mootch.
Below: Mustang 6117 waits for a new life in a BLM adoption pen.

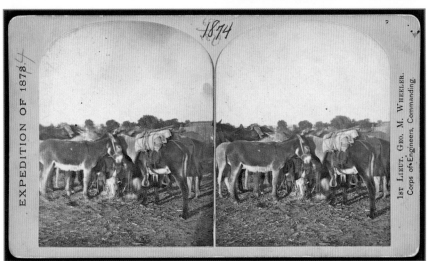

Timothy O'Sullivan, Burro Pack Team, 1874.

Bats Chiroptera

God loves bats and you should too. Worldwide, one in five mammals is a bat, and they range from microbats the size of a silver dollar all the way up to Australian fruit bats with six-foot wingspans. Some catch fish and others specialize in tracking down singing frogs; one bat in Baja can survive by drinking seawater. California has twenty-six bat species and they pollinate agaves, gobble mosquitoes by the hour, and even hunt moths over downtown Los Angeles. While they do live in caves and abandoned mines, bats also roost in palms, in the cracks of tree bark, and under bridges. They are not mice—ignore the name in German, *Fledermaus*—and they don't get in your hair, turn people into vampires, or spread rabies any more often than your dog does. They are also not blind, and if you hold one, most kinds are as soft and silky as a kitten.

A bat's wing is its hand, just lightened, elongated, and enhanced with a durable but thin membrane. Many mammal species glide, but only bats can truly fly (and some for long-distance migrations). Everything is stripped down for action: small body, fierce mouth, state-of-the-art radar. As Diane Ackerman points out, "Adult bats don't weigh much. They're mainly fur and appetite."

Bats hunt with a combination of eyesight and ultrasonic pulses. A device attached to your smartphone can make bat hunting calls both visible and audible: I have stood on a pedestrian bridge in Santa Cruz and stared at the readout on

California leaf-nosed bat.

Bats live not only in caves and belfries but also roost in abandoned mines, under bridges, and inside hollow trees.
Left: When it came time for ears, the spotted bat went back for seconds.

my phone, awed as dozens of Yuma myotis and Mexican free-tailed bats strafed the creek below, as busy and efficient as the best *Top Gun* aces. Nearby, the evening traffic honked and tailgated on Highway 1, the drivers oblivious to the feeding frenzy just beneath their windows.

Besides creeks in Santa Cruz, Mexican (or Brazilian) free-tailed bats are the ones you can see at Carlsbad Caverns National Park and also emerging in a funnel cloud from the Congress Avenue Bridge in Austin. Closer to home, you can find them under bridges near Davis. They have a long list of "wow" attributes. Some people are surprised to learn that this bat (a) forms the largest colonies of any mammal, (b) lives in gaseous environments that would kill most other animals, (c) flies up to 10,000 feet high, (d) is faster than a cheetah (up to 100 mph—

Humans shouldn't be so scared of bats; bats should be scared of humans.
—Merlin Tuttle

even faster than a peregrine falcon in level flight), (e) adopts orphans, and (f) forms clusters that can include up to five hundred pups in a single square foot of cave roof. If you were able to have a pet bat, it probably would outlive all your dogs. Some banded bats have been recaptured twenty to thirty-five years later. One myotis remained in excellent health when last seen at forty-one years of age. According to ecologist Merlin Tuttle, this is the equivalent of a hundred-year-old human still being able to run sprints through an obstacle course.

Above and below right: Pallid bat. Above right: Hoary bat.

Other fab California bats include our largest one, the western mastiff, which has a two-foot wingspan and calls audible to humans. Deserts, mountains, coastal plains: you can expect it from Lava Beds National Monument (a great place for all kinds of bats) down to the tip of Point Loma in San Diego. It is active year-round; I've seen them in December over the Los Angeles River.

The spotted bat has pink ears and pink wings and a black-and-white body like a panda shrink-rayed to the size of a starling. If this bat were the size of us, its ears would be bigger than tennis rackets. The pallid bat has a sixteen-inch wingspan and is pale yellow. It eats crickets and scorpions, plucking them right off the ground. Foraging in desert scrub can tear up their wings—most animals, seen close, show some wear and tear, and if you track a pallid bat with your binoculars as it's backlit against the sky, sometimes you can see these holes as little pinpoints of dancing twilight.

And here Alice began to get rather sleepy, and went on saying to herself, in a dreamy sort of way, "Do cats eat bats? Do cats eat bats?" and sometimes, "Do bats eat cats?"
—*Lewis Carroll,* Alice's Adventures in Wonderland

Collectively, bats eat tons and tons of insects every night and are found in all California habitats, from Golden Gate Park to Mount Whitney. Many animals can try to claim the tiara as being the most misunderstood, but bats are certainly first among equals in this. That's a shame, since as these photos show, they are diverse, surprising, and, in their own way, as beautiful as your own pets (or, in the case of most pugs, more so).

Coyote *Canis latrans*

What eats avocados, tennis shoes, and house cats, looks like a slimmed-down wolf, wails like a "dismal ventriloquist" (Teddy Roosevelt), observes family values, walks on tippy toes, runs at forty miles an hour, and lives in fifty-eight out of California's fifty-eight counties? The answer is the same song dog who has a black-tipped tail from stealing fire and who in most stories wants to make off with your wife. Cities don't stop them: there are at least a hundred coyotes living just inside the city of San Francisco alone. From tide pools to feedlots to the bristlecone pines (and from Arcata to Zzyzx) coyotes adapt and survive, dodging traps, raising families, and yip-yip-yipping in solidarity with fire-truck sirens.

Coyotes can hunt solo or, over carrion or other bounties, form a solid pack. Scent-marking along territorial boundaries helps everybody know who's in the mood for love, who is related to whom, and just where the *Keep Out* signs start and stop. There are such things as coydog hybrids—*maybe*. Generally speaking, dogs and coyotes don't get along, and without measuring the skulls of dead specimens, hybrid status is a hard claim to prove.

What we do know is that C-144, a radio-collared female coyote, not only manages to live full time in downtown Los Angeles, ranging between Echo Park and Koreatown, but that she successfully raised a litter of pups and has crossed and recrossed the Hollywood Freeway. Do they ever attack people? Not usually, but if people feed them, boundaries get a bit blurred. You're a lot more likely to be bitten by a random dog (or to die from being kicked by a cow) than to come to harm from a coyote. For one thing, you're way bigger and way heavier—most coyotes weigh from seventeen to forty pounds—and let's face it, humans are loud, unpredictable, and stink of aftershave…would *you* want to saunter over and have a bite? Most coyotes stay well clear and for good reason.

With wolves turning up now in California, how do we tell them from coyotes? Assuming they're not vocalizing (a coyote sounds like a wolf who has just had a snort of helium), then check the ears: coyotes have taller, pointier ears. Also look carefully at the snout (longer in a coyote). And the shoulders and chest are a bit less robust in a coyote, less like a beefy sled dog and more like the chaparral escape artist that it is. Of course, it can be

Coyotes, cockroaches, and sonnets will always be with us.
—Charles Wright

hard to tell them apart in winter, when thicker pelts obscure contours, an excuse coyote hunters in other states use every time they "accidentally" kill a wolf. As several editorials have pointed out, that's an easy mistake to prevent: let's just outlaw coyote hunting completely and let wolves and coyotes and coydogs and bears and bobcats and all the carnivores just carry on as nature intended.

Gray Wolf *Canis lupus*

A folk legend about wolves tells that when a wolf and a man meet, should the wolf see the man first, the man will fall mute. Perhaps readers of this book will have a chance to test this for themselves, now that the wolf is once more a resident of California. Last reported in 1924, wolves seemed gone for good, but in 2011, a single wolf, OR-7, wandered into California, lighting up environmentalists and the general media with equal excitement. California has recently had two separate wolf packs, the Lassen Pack and the Shasta Pack, and a single wolf was seen in 2018 near Lake Tahoe. The general who-begat-whom is well known: OR-7 originally came from a pack in Oregon (hence his name), and Oregon's wolves had come from Idaho, and Idaho's wolves had been transplanted from Canada. Unless you're a wolf hater—and there are a surprising number of them still around—this represents a fabulously encouraging success story.

Certainly California *had* wolves, once upon a time. Black, white, gray—reports came from all over the state, and DNA evidence indicates that the wolves in Southern California were lobos, or the Mexican gray wolf, a desert-adapted subspecies of the larger, better-known timber wolf (which is also called the Rocky Mountain wolf). As with grizzly bears, it would be great if we had had a thorough ecological review before the last ones disappeared. What was average pack size?

Lobos, or Mexican gray wolves (left) used to live in the southern deserts of the state, while timber wolves ranged north of that.

How did they respond to drought? What was the interaction of wolves, coyotes, bears, and mountain lions around kill sites? Yellowstone and Denali National Parks give us glimpses of lost California, but accurate, firsthand reports would be great to find. Gray wolves have been unearthed at the La Brea Tar Pits, but more common among fossils found there is its larger cousin, the dire wolf, extinct as of 10,000 years ago. It must have been abundant, since so far scientists have cataloged 200,000 dire wolf specimens, representing 4,000 individuals.

Wolves are highly social and cooperative hunters, and they can take down an elk in ways a brace of coyotes couldn't manage in their wildest Charles Atlas dreams. As puny but perhaps tasty bundles of meat, should humans be worried? Probably not. In the past hundred years, pet wolves killed two people total, rabid wolves two more, habituated garbage dump wolves one person, and truly wild, natural wolves a total of two people, both in Alaska. That sounds like a lot, but in the US, 10,000 people a year are killed by drunk drivers. We also average fifty lightning deaths a year, often around golf courses. If you're worried about safety, forget wolves and close all bars at 7:00 p.m.

The wolf exerts a powerful influence on the human imagination. It takes your stare and turns it back on you.

—Barry Lopez

Also, be sure to boycott golf courses: you are much more likely to die from being hit in the head by a golf ball than to have an unpleasant encounter with a wolf.

Given that ranchers have the legal right to shoot a wolf accused of taking sheep and cattle—something that has already happened recently—and given, too, the coyote hunters who "accidentally" blast wolves, California's wolves have a lot more to fear from us than we do from them.

Gray Fox and Red Fox

Urocyon cinereoargenteus and *Vulpes vulpes*

Gray foxes are smaller and less doglike than coyotes, and occur in forests, meadows, edgelands, and chaparral. Around farms and ranches they will den under outbuildings, and they turn up on trail cameras in the Baldwin Hills, almost within sight of LAX. One of the best places to see them is Point Reyes. The gray fox can climb trees (the only wild dog in North America to do so), and it eats rodents, birds, frogs, insects, berries, and fruit. This is the sister species to the island fox and both show a mix of salt-and-pepper backs with a cinnamon neck and a broad, raccoon-shaped face. The tail is long and bushy and black-tipped, and the legs seem short at first, at least until the fox catches your scent and you see how swiftly it gallops away.

The red fox is an eastern species introduced into much of California (or escaped from fur farms), with a small additional population native to the Sierra and in the Sacramento Valley. It is longer-legged than a gray fox, and is normally all-red, with black lower legs and a white-tipped (not black-tipped) tail. This is the same fox as in Aesop's *Fables* and it lives in Europe, Alaska, and the Himalayas—indeed, it is the most widespread carnivore in the world.

Are foxes magnetic? Red foxes are well studied, and like coyotes, they hunt for voles in winter by listening intently, bunching up, and then springing into the air and punching through the snowpack with front legs, ready to grab a very startled dinner. (This pause-and-leap is called mousing.) Collating data from

Most red foxes were introduced (or escaped from fur farms), but some in the Sierra and around Sacramento are native. This one near Hayward has caught a jackrabbit. Bottom left and right: Gray fox adult and pup.

many hundreds of observations, we now know that successful red foxes orient their attacks in line with the earth's magnetic poles. The current hypothesis is that this helps them micro-tune depth perception, so they know precisely how deep the snow is before they pounce.

Gray foxes occur from Washington down through the prairies and forests to Mexico, Central America, and the top crescent of South America. So far as taxonomy

Be like the fox
who makes more tracks than necessary,
some in the wrong direction.
—Wendell Berry

votes now, that one animal is the same species through all those lines of latitude, though if the gray fox were some other animal (a yellow warbler for example, or a herring gull) you can bet it would be dialed up as three or five or ten different species. For now, it is transnational and polymorphic, just doing its fox thing from border to border and life to life, a lingering symbol of unity in an otherwise Balkanized world.

Island Fox *Urocyon littoralis*

Endemic to California, the island fox is the smallest wild dog in North America. Unless you're a lighthouse keeper or National Park Service ranger, the island fox is a case of you going to it, not it coming to you, since you need a boat to get to its home range. Gray and cinnamon and infinitely curious, it is basically a regular gray fox evolved down to be as small as a house cat. Found on six of the eight Channel Islands, the fox is easiest to encounter on Santa Cruz. You also have good odds for seeing lots of common dolphins on the boat ride over from Ventura, and one lucky mammal watcher even once found a stray Guadalupe fur seal on the beach when he got there. Birders take note: this is a twofer, since Santa Cruz Island also hosts the endemic island scrub-jay.

Twenty years ago, it was not clear that the fox would survive. Bald eagles eat fish (not foxes), and bald eagles keep golden eagles from nesting, but due to DDT's ill effects, by the 1980s bald eagles had almost completely disappeared from the Channel Islands. The golden eagles that replaced them *do* eat mammals, and they soon began to decimate fox populations. With DDT banned, fish stocks became less lethal for higher-end predators. Bald eagles were able to come back, boosted by habitat restoration and golden eagle relocation programs. With the remnant fox populations supplemented by captive-bred releases, the foxes came back too.

Now if you go to a place like Scorpion Anchorage on Santa Cruz Island, you can see a dozen or more foxes in one day, watching them hop up on picnic tables or poke inquisitive noses into backpacks. Leave a pack unattended for five minutes and they'll find a way in, ready to help themselves to all your grapes or potato chips or Fig Newtons—that is, they will try doing that until a raven shows up and bogarts the treasure for itself.

Biologists use the term "insular dwarfism" to explain small body sizes in constrained habitat. The Channel Islands had a spectacular example of that in the case of the pygmy mammoth, a miniature version of the regular Ice Age mam-

moth that first swam over from the mainland when sea levels were lower. As glaciers melted and sea levels rose, the island-bound mammoths evolved to be smaller (and to need less food). A typical mainland mammoth stood fourteen feet high at the shoulders, while the dwarf mammoth was between four and eight feet...more the size of a small Clydesdale than the megafauna of the Pleistocene. (How much would you pay to see the Budweiser wagon parade past you, pulled by mammoths, not horses?)

Evolution loves death more than it loves you or me. This is easy to write, easy to read, and hard to believe. The words are simple, the concept clear—but you don't believe it, do you? Nor do I. How could I, when we're both so lovable?

—Annie Dillard

Island foxes are an example of dwarfism, and they too arrived on their own (rafting across perhaps on mats of flood-surge vegetation), but they also got a boost when the Chumash carried them from northern islands like San Miguel to the southern islands like Santa Catalina. This movement helped keep gene pools robust as well. You can see them in captivity at the Santa Barbara Zoo, the Los Angeles Zoo, or stuffed and on display at the visitor center in Ventura, but as with so many things in life, they always are more interesting when seen wild and in person (especially if it's not your picnic lunch they've just made off with).

Kit Fox _Vulpes macrotis_

This slender fox is a dryland species found in the Great Basin and Mexico; it is closely related to the swift fox of the Great Plains. In California kit foxes live in deserts and arid scrubland, including Death Valley, Anza-Borrego, the Salton Sea, and in the San Joaquin Valley, where there is an endangered subspecies. The Carrizo Plain provides prime habitat for pronghorn and badgers, and for this compact predator also. Before urban development the kit fox would have occurred in Southern California along the coastal plain, but the last record was 1931.

If there wasn't already a bat-eared fox in Africa, that would make a great common name: the kit fox hunts kangaroo rats, rabbits, and crickets, and it does so using ears so big they nearly meet at the midpoint of its forehead. (Another name could be long-tailed fox, since the tail is 40 percent of the total body length.) Kit foxes use burrows year-round, often on a small mound or knoll, with several entrances and a scattering of bones and feathers to indicate what's in season right now. It's a vocal species and reference books provide lists of its noises that include an orchestra of yaps, barks, growls, purrs, croaks, and snarls. Like other dogs, they scent-mark with urine and feces; the poo of a large kit fox and a small coyote can be hard to tell apart, at least for us. One assumes the canids themselves have no trouble.

You may well ask, "Yes, but how can I see one of these critters myself?" Nature often surprises us with its adaptability. One night I was coming out of a meeting at California State University, Bakersfield, and there he was: a bold and casual kit fox, working his way through the parking lot, scent-marking each and every truck tire. It turns out, this is one of thirty of the endangered San Joaquin Valley kit foxes that lives on the campus grounds. Safer from coyotes and bobcats inside city limits than out in the countryside, this group is part of four hundred to five hundred kit foxes that live inside the city limits of Bakersfield.

Wonder is the heaviest element on the periodic table. Even a tiny fleck of it stops time.

—Diane Ackerman

As Creedence Clearwater Revival sings in "Lookin' out my back door," while listening to Buck Owens—a classic Bakersfield thing to do—you can "Look at all the happy creatures dancing on the lawn."

Sounds like a great way to spend a summer night.

American Black Bear *Ursus americanus*

From sea level to the Sierra crest, black bears handle all environments except pure desert, relying on intelligence, curiosity, and the arm strength of a squad of linebackers to traverse mountains, dig out squirrels, and fillet ant-filled trees. In the "scrimmage of appetite" (Delmore Schwartz) bears also eat spring grass and windfall apples, dead deer and ripe garbage, darting trout and swarming termites, plus a Home Town Buffet of acorns and mushrooms and beehives and baby birds, and even the birds' own birdseed—metal birdseed cage and all.

Our bears usually weigh one hundred to three hundred pounds. (A stuffed bear now on display in a window in Bishop was supposedly six hundred twenty pounds.) Colors vary from dirty blond to cinnamon to Elvira black. In the wild, bears live twenty years, and all bears have noses a hundred times more acute than ours, one reason it's important to store food in bear lockers when parked overnight. Black bears can climb trees, swim rivers, and crush elk bones to get at the marrow. And not to alarm you—bears really don't want to cause a fuss—but all bears, even fat, sleepy ones, can outrun you by at least ten miles an hour. If you see one hiking, keep your distance and let the bear carry on being a bear. Leash pets and children. If it approaches, make sure it has an escape route, and shout, wave your arms, and act large. (Don't play dead unless you're in Alaska and it's not a black bear but a grizzly.)

If you visited Yosemite or Sequoia National Parks from the 1920s to the 1950s, you had a chance to see a "bear show." Rangers collected garbage cans of scraps from tent camps and lodges, and each night delivered this to central viewing areas, which sometimes even had grandstands and spotlights. (Other times just car headlights provided the stadium lighting.) After dumping the garbage, the head ranger would bang his shovel on his truck, telling bears it was show time. The lights would come up and visitors got the thrill of seeing a dozen bears at once in their (un)natural habitat, chowing down on kitchen scraps.

Nowadays we know better, and in most parks problem bears are darted, tagged, and hazed if they show too little terror around the nastiest predator on the planet (us). It turns out, giving bears a one-way helicopter ride into the backcountry doesn't really work: it only takes them a few days to saunter back to where they started, and it's not as if there are empty parts of the landscape that don't already have bears (and bear territories) filling the map. Training bears to avoid people works better, as does training people not to leave food unattended. Remember: "A fed bear is a dead bear," and ultimately any habituated bear will probably end up shot.

Bears of course hibernate in winter, except when they don't. If there's abundant food, the need to wait for spring lessens, and winter food can be provided by a forest floor covered with acorns if the snows are late, or, at Lake Tahoe or Mammoth, it may be trash if homeowners don't keep their bins locked tight. Female

bears are more inclined to hibernate than males, since they give birth in the den and the young need time to develop before encountering the world.

We humans may be sad that grizzly bears are gone, but black bears most certainly are not: the departure of grizzlies opens up opportunities for other, smaller ursids—and black bears have filled this niche. In Southern California the spread of black bears was sped up by intentional introduction in the 1930s (though odds are, they would have come on their own anyway). This population hibernates even less often than the Sierra residents do, and, if TV news coverage is to be believed, these SoCal bears especially like paddling around swimming pools in Monrovia and eating Costco meatballs in Glendale.

Some days you have to work hard to save the bear. Some days the bear will save you.
—Barbara Kingsolver

In many indigenous cosmologies bears inhabit a liminal space—part animal, part human. If you meet a bear, traditions suggest introducing yourself in your most respectful, formal language. No matter which tribal affiliation you most identify with, this seems like good advice for almost all our encounters with the natural world.

Grizzly Bear *Ursus arctos*

Originally widespread in prairies, foothills, and mountains, grizzly bears were once a major component of wild California. Wouldn't you love to step out of a time machine in Monterey, let's say on a winter morning in the 1750s, and be able to watch grizzly bears and condors side by side, feasting on a beached whale? (There were jaguars in California then too.) The California grizzly was the same hump-shouldered, broad-muzzled giant that still lives in Alaska, where it is also called the brown bear. Besides walking right to left across the state flag, the grizzly bear also lingers on today as our state prehistoric artifact, coming to that status via a stone carving, 8,000 years old, discovered in San Diego in 1985.

All accounts agree this species was initially abundant, just as all accounts agree that the bears were hunted out with profligate efficiency. Reducing a population of 10,000 bears to nil took just 75 years. We can almost hear the clock ticking down: San Diego, last one shot in 1899; Orange County, 1908; Tujunga Wash, Los Angeles, 1916; and the final few, Sequoia National Park, one shot in 1922, and the last of the last of the last glimpsed in the autumn of 1924.

Our local grizzly subspecies was *Ursus arctos californicus*, but careful studies were not carried out when the population was still viable, so not a lot is known about the details of its life and habits. Here's what we have so far. Size? Huge (maybe a thousand pounds). Food? Acorns, blackberries, deer, frogs, grapes, grass, grubs, honey, manzanita berries, mice, mushrooms,

the offal from tanneries, pine nuts, rose hips, salmon, squirrels, tule roots, wild oats, willow bark, and yellow jackets. Pace? Slow and deliberate: as the biggest land animal in North America, what's the rush? Sociability? Yes, lots of reports of ten or fifteen at once. Hibernation? Apparently not often.

They made a tremendous impression on Natives and Europeans alike, and we remember bears in our place names, from Big Bear Lake above San Bernardino to the many variations on Los Osos ("the bears"), which has been applied to mountains, beaches, rivers, hotels, condos, and riparian canyons.

Do we ever want grizzlies back, at least a little bit? Yes and no. The fact that they were large and visible made them particular targets, here as elsewhere. By simple math, apex predators occur at lower densities than smaller carnivore species, making them more vulnerable to extinction. If they had lasted into the present day, would we be better at management? We would like to say "Yes," but it may not be such a sure bet. Many animals are easier to be nostalgic about in hindsight.

If you have ever seen those video clips of black bears breaking into cars in Yosemite, their fat butts sticking out of a passenger window while head and torso wreck the interior, we might have second thoughts about an animal so powerful it could try to tip over a Humvee or pull the Yosemite food lockers right off their foundations. Certainly, our current black bears want nothing to do with grizzlies, whose top dawg status kept these smaller bears benched on the ecological sidelines.

Relegating grizzlies to Alaska is about like relegating happiness to heaven; one may never get there.

—Aldo Leopold

On the other hand, a wilderness without drama, without major players, seems diminished somehow. The backcountry may be marginally safer, but it also feels incomplete. "Rich country, rich soil," writes Rick Bass, "yields great and rich animals, which yield great and rich stories—which yield great cultures." Or as Werner Herzog put it, "What would an ocean be without a monster lurking in the dark? It would be like sleep without dreams."

Raccoon and Ringtail

Procyon lotor and *Bassariscus astutus*

"Raccoon" is an Algonquian word that slid into English even earlier than the words "coyote" and "chocolate." Some prefer to use a less kind name: trash panda. No matter what we call it, this is a mostly nocturnal, water-associated, stripe-tailed, hunch-butted, bandit-masked survivor, weighing five or ten (or twenty or twenty-five) pounds. Bigger than a cat and usually smaller than a midsized dog, it out-clevers both and likes to eat anything we like and a bit more besides: animal, vegetable, or mineral, it will have a go. One favorite food is crayfish (or in your family do y'all say crawdads?), but it's broadly omnivorous. Sensitive paws have great dexterity; raccoons don't really wash their food first, but they do manipulate new things to see what's the best part to eat.

Creeks, ditches, and mucky culverts are good places to look for raccoons, or at least that's where their distinctive tracks will show that they've patrolled recently. Habitat can include coastal marshes with very few trees or woodlands with hardly any streams, and just about every city park, sewage pond, and storm drain in between. From San Francisco to the Everglades, raccoons navigate the urban interface better than almost any other wild animal. Only rats and coyotes may be their equal.

Like a raccoon, a ringtail (left) has a black-and-white tail, but it is slimmer, rarer, and mostly found along cliffs or in treetops. Above: An urban marsh, prime raccoon habitat.

Climbing in Joshua Tree or driving late at night through Yosemite (especially along the Merced River near El Portal) you may also encounter a slimmer animal with a taste for cliff-scampering. The ringtail—sometimes inappropriately called ringtail cat—has a striped tail too, but its tail is longer and more lemur-like, and this animal always dashes and scampers, unlike the waddle and galumph of a typical raccoon. Another name for a ringtail is cacomistle, though that term better applies to a sister species in the tropics.

America has endured two fashion fads centered on raccoons. Fess Parker as Daniel Boone made the schoolboys of the sixties covet coonskin caps—a furry fez with a dangling tail. Before that, in the Roaring Twenties, it was young men and fur coats. The song "Doin' the Raccoon" includes the lyrics, "From every college campus comes the cheer: oy-yoy! / The season for the raccoon coat is here, my boy!" Japan had its own raccoon craze, due to a 1977 cartoon series, *Rascal the Raccoon*. Kids wanted the real thing, so importers brought pets to Japan. As always happens, they escaped and are now pests. (They live in Europe, too.)

If you will, Lord, make me the teeth
hot in the mouth of a raccoon scraping
the junk I scraped from last night's plates,
make me the blue eye of that young crow cocked to
me—too selfish to even look up from the black
of my damn phone.

—*Nickole Brown*

It's hard not to imagine astronauts returning to the moon, and while they set up the space dome and the space kitchen, we'll see a sly, black-masked face peeking out, glass bell helmet full of pure air, as the first raccoon in outer space decides which garbage bin to raid first.

Striped Skunk *Mephitis mephitis*

According to a report from 1906, the anal fluid of a skunk, "much diluted and administered internally," has proved efficacious "as a remedy for asthma, whooping cough, and croup." Is this a case of the cure being worse than the disease? De-scented skunks used to be kept as pets in California, but now, like tigers, hedgehogs, and machine guns, they are illegal. States differ in tolerating odd choices: West Virginia and Florida still allow folks to keep a pet skunk, but while you may own a tiger in West Virginia, it can't be walked in public (even on leash), plus whistling underwater is illegal there, so maybe no state in the Union is truly perfect.

As for the beast itself, we've probably all seen one—they thrive in and around farms, ranches, marshes, parks, and coastal cities—or, if you've not seen one even as roadkill ("What's black and white and red all over?"), you almost certainly will have smelled one, since the stink lingers for days. Stripes vary in width but in this species are always boldly black and white—a warning to other animals to stay away. Even a coyote will back off in a face-off with a skunk.

Skunks eat fruit, insects, mice, garbage, and grubs—true omnivores, so if they can nose it out, dig it up, or chase it down, they'll have a try. Nocturnal and ground based, they don't climb trees, but they will burrow under houses. Robert Lowell in his poem "Skunk Hour" equates them with survival; he contrasts sterile mansions and Bostonian money with the strength of a midnight skunk and its "moonstruck eyes [of] red fire."

Inset: The spotted skunk is smaller than the striped skunk and always shows swirly white lines.

We have a second one to watch for as well. Smaller and shyer than the main kind, the spotted skunk looks like somebody got frustrated and scribbled its stripes in a mad rush, since they zigzag back and forth or just look like big white dots. Striped skunks are city dwellers, but spotted skunks stay in chaparral and coastal scrub (like in Yosemite and at Point Reyes); they also live in the Channel Islands, but not the open desert.

Besides being home to our same two kinds, Arizona hosts two more species, the hooded skunk and the hog-nosed skunk. Does that make them twice as lucky as we are, or twice as cursed? It is true a skunk can move its glands, so it can aim, plus it can send out its stink ray at least ten feet. What should you do if you have the misfortune to be zapped? The Internet is full of folk remedies, but the best solution may be to burn your clothes, take a bath in a mix of hydrogen peroxide and baking soda, and then move into a motel for a week. During that time if you find your whooping cough is suddenly getting better, be sure to email the AMA.

There is no magic line between the wild and the urban.

—Greg Pauly

Feral Cat *Felis catus*

America, I love you, but as your best friend I need to talk to you about your cat problem. You have become the proverbial cat lady, except instead of forty-eight cats in a one-bedroom, sagging-porch house, you keep yours in nature and there are a *lot*. How many? Somewhere between 50 million and 100 million. Los Angeles County alone has 2 million feral cats.

The problem is that cats eat birds, as in a *billion* a year (billion with a *b*)—unless it's a number even larger than that. And at the wildland-urban interface, they're nailing everything else too, including frogs and snakes and small mammals like the endangered Stephens's kangaroo rat. A feral cat's Latin name should be "serial killer." Equally culpable are household pets allowed to be outside cats part of the day (or night). Muffy or Mr. Wiggles leads a double life: cozy and nap-drunk at home, but a Voldemort-sponsored Death Eater once set loose upon the world. In San Diego, one study showed that a patch of remnant habitat surrounded by 100 houses—houses with the usual number of pet cats—lost 840 rodents a year, 525 birds, and 595 lizards. Few environments can sustain that quantity of daily, year-round harassment.

Wild cats were once wildcats (note the spelling), a still-extant species pair in Europe and Africa, *Felis silvestris* and *Felis lybica*. As humans transitioned from being gatherer-hunters to grower-gatherers, the townies' stored grain attracted mice and mice attracted cats, and the pet trade was born. There is only the slimmest genetic difference between a feral cat and its wildcat elders, and in general, from a snow leopard to an ocelot to a back-fence tomcat, all felids share the same body plan. Individual species may only be a million or two years old, but the cat lineage goes back 20 million years. No wonder they eat so many birds: they've been doing it for ten times longer than hominids have been on the planet.

Actually, I don't hate cats. I am just kind of afraid of them.
—Clay Aiken

If you love cats, keep them indoors. They will live twice as long, they won't endure a miserable burden of ticks, mites, and fleas, they won't get (and spread) toxoplasmosis, and they won't be depopulating the world of warblers, juncos, sparrows, towhees, bluebirds, and robins.

The African (top left) and European (top right) wildcats are ancestors to the two feral housecats shown below.

Bobcat *Lynx rufus*

In a state bursting with superlatives—the tallest trees, the biggest whales, the most expensive houses—it's easy to overlook the bobcat, which is basically the Tom Hanks of the natural world. Not flashy, not ostentatious, no sex, drugs, and rock 'n' roll. Instead, it represents durability and a quiet, enduring presence—the everyman of carnivores.

Identification is straightforward. Compared to a cat or feral dog, a bobcat is always longer legged and pointier eared, and despite its apparent size, it's more bantamweight than many would guess. Adult bobcats can weigh as little as fifteen pounds, and in California rarely go past twenty-five. Seen well, the face has a Civil War look, with old-fashioned sideburns framing the face in black and white. The pelt varies from beige to gray to reddish blond and is usually spotted, though not darkly so. Mostly the bobcat just wants to blend in. "Who am I? Oh don't mind me, I'm nobody."

As the boreal forests become more fragmented, bobcats are replacing their larger lynx cousins in southern Canada, but, precontact, bobcats were mostly found in the Lower 48 and Northern Mexico. That range remains true today, with a missing patch only in the most intensely cultivated parts of the Midwest. In Mexico it occurs as far south as Oaxaca but not any deeper into the tropics. All bobcats are strictly meat eaters ("obligate carnivores"), so unlike coyotes or skunks, they never snack on manzanita berries or raid garbage pails. What they specialize in is the rabbit clan, which can make up to 70 percent of their diet. They also eat game birds and henhouse chickens, mice and rats and voles, gophers and lizards and squirrels and beavers, and will even risk scavenging a dead deer if a mountain lion has momentarily left one unattended.

As the genus name reveals, a bobcat is a scrubland lynx, scaled down a bit from the others, true, but at home in a baker's dozen habitats, from oaks, pines, and deserts, right up to the edges of our largest cities. They were thriving in Griffith Park long before the mountain lion named P-22 ever showed up, and they will still be there after that superstar cat has passed into myth and legend. They don't occur on the Channel Islands, but anywhere else it would be hard to draw a twenty-mile circle and not intersect a bobcat's territory. Forgoing the wolf pack's chilling howls and the shark's iconic top fin, the bobcat is so modest he's nearly invisible.

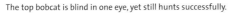
The top bobcat is blind in one eye, yet still hunts successfully.

The hardest thing in the world is to simplify your life; it's so easy to make it complex.
—Yvon Chouinard

The common name comes from the bobbed or shortened tail. Where did the rest of the tail go? Just don't need them. Tails are handy for balance when climbing trees (which they do, but not regularly) and for using as a rudder in hard braking (like a cheetah), but in thickets and scrubland they just get in the way. Similarly, midsized cats like Africa's caracal and serval also have abbreviated tails, as do the world's other three lynx species—Canadian lynx, Eurasian lynx, and Spain's endangered Iberian lynx.

Some people do still hunt bobcats, with a take in California of about 250 animals a year, but most of us want to look at them, not shoot them. Good places to try include Point Reyes National Seashore, any of the desert parks, Yosemite Valley in winter, and the foothills east of Pinnacles National Park.

Mountain Lion *Puma concolor*

Also called the puma or cougar, the mountain lion is a New World species found from Alaska right down to the bottom end of Patagonia, and from Death Valley to the frigid summits of the Andes. In California, the puma is more talked about than seen, but since sport hunting was banned in 1990, mountain lion populations have continued to recover—we may not have any grizzly bears, but we almost certainly have many thousands of mountain lions, and they surprise hikers or startle drivers even quite close to the city.

How close? In Los Angeles, the urban island of Griffith Park has a resident mountain lion, the famous P-22, who was still alive as we went to press. Puma-22 was only discovered when Miguel Ordeñana, now a biologist with the Natural History Museum of Los Angeles County, was checking his camera traps as part of the Griffith Park Connectivity Study to see how the park's wide-ranging mammal populations were able to enter and exit the seemingly isolated park. We can imagine the answer, on the day of discovery: "Doing fine, thank you, except Holy Moses, that's not a bobcat, that's a you-know-what." It has become so iconic some people even have P-22 tattoos.

Who can blame them? His story is one of astounding tenacity and survival. He hero'd his way across two major freeways, and we all admire his ability to overcome urban obstacles and coexist with humans in an unprecedentedly small territory—only nine square miles compared to the usual two hundred.

In Spanish this animal is *león* or just *puma*, but among regional variations, it's hard to top Edward Hoagland's "deer tiger." He's also helpful when it comes to transcribing the calls, noting that "when conversing with their mates [mountain lions] coo like pigeons, sob like women, emit a flat slight shriek, a popping bubbling growl, or mew, or yowl." To fill out his concert, Hoagland says

that pumas also "growl and suddenly caterwaul into falsetto." Another fact to mention at parties: mountain lions can't roar but they can purr. (Only big cats can roar, the members of the genus *Panthera*.)

Kittens have spots (and, briefly, piercing blue eyes) but adults are yellow eyed and plain brown; males are larger than females (and will eat kittens if they're not his). All mountain lions have long tails—some people manage to mistake bobcats for pumas, which really is an epic fail at your woodcraft. Color, length, and tail: nothing in the mountains is like it. Compared to African lions, pumas are slimmer and lighter; they are solo hunters who like to leap on prey from above or behind, breaking the neck or suffocating the target animal. They sure win the gold medal for jumping: twenty to twenty-five feet horizontally, and forty feet vertically. That's not as long as a city bus, but it's not much short of it, either.

> The easiest predator to know is the predator within us.
>
> —Elena Passarello

Frank Stephens, an early naturalist, reported that "the flesh of cougars is said to look and taste like veal." Usually, though, it is the puma that does the eating, and its preferred three-course meal starts and ends with deer, and in California, mule deer provide 90 percent of the diet. But it will eat any other animal it can catch, including gray foxes, rabbits, sea lion pups, and raccoons. Attacks on humans are possible but very rare. If you see one on the trail, look big, act fierce, and whatever you do, don't turn and run—that triggers their attack mode.

Most of us would be glad for even a glimpse, and so would accept a fair bit of risk in exchange for the electric shock of the experience. If you hike a lot and still have not come across one, odds are, a mountain lion saw you first and ghosted away into the brush. To have a top predator living so close among us provides what Dana Goodyear calls "Paleo for the soul." Even if you don't see one often (or ever), it is still a great solace to know they are out there in the dark, a gorgeous cat and a lethal killer, another awesome component of nature's grand design.

Sea Otter *Enhydra lutris*

Sea otters are the patron saints of Monterey Bay, and as they float on their backs, cracking open sea urchins on flat pieces of rock balanced on their tummies, whiskery faces scrunched up in concentration, it's hard not to worship them as the ne plus ultra of cuteness. Sea otters lack a seal's layer of blubber, so it takes a lot of food to stoke their roaring furnaces. On average, a sea otter spends 20 to 50 percent of the day foraging, during which it will consume 20 to 25 percent of its body mass in food. Of course, those figures still leave half the day for snoozing in the kelp or grooming their fur or just frolicking about in a winsome way, and it takes a bleak imagination indeed to go back to those days—not so very long ago—when they were so thoroughly hunted for their fur that they were presumed extinct.

It's a special fur, we have to grant our forefathers that—densest of any animal on earth, with the widely reported fact that it has one million hairs per square inch. (Somebody send out the interns to do a recount and verify that, please.) Females weigh fifty pounds and males up to seventy, and at four feet long, they do offer a reasonably good-sized pelt. The Russians thought so, anyway, and in the eighteenth and nineteenths centuries worked their way down the Pacific coast, cleaning out the otters cove after cove, Alaska down to Baja. Yet they missed some—not many, but enough—and in 1938 science finally figured out what the

locals knew all along, that a few lingered around Big Sur. Now the sea otter population centers on a rocky (and scenic) stretch of coast from San Mateo County to Morro Bay. Out of concern about an oil spill or some other stroke of super bad luck, some sea otters were relocated to Catalina. It has kelp and abalone and nice weather and attractive, rocky coves. It should have been perfect, but the sea otters bobbed up out of the water, took a look around, said, "Wait a minute, this isn't Monterey!"—and promptly swam back home.

They eat crabs and shellfish, part of the checks and balances of intertidal life. Otters eat the crabs that would otherwise eat the sea slugs that then couldn't eat the algae that would then smother the eelgrass, and so on up and down the chain of life. Sea otters also eat sea urchins (which can quickly mow down the kelp forest), which is the prime reason they are considered to be a keystone species. And yet nature has a dark

> *Animals give us their constant, unjaded faces, and we burden them with our bodies and civilized ordeals.*
>
> —*Gretel Ehrlich*

side too: in mating, male otters basically rape the females and sometimes even kill seal pups. Oh, say it ain't so, Joe. (No wonder they're called the wolverines of the sea.) Welcome to thug life: another survey reports that "male sea otters will kidnap sea otter pups and hold them underwater until the female gives up her food. This happens often enough to get its own term: 'hostage behavior.'"

This reminds us that terms like "cute" or "mean" do not belong in the natural world: sea otters just do as natural selection intended, which is to live otter lives according to otter rules. In Peru and Chile there's a look-alike species called the marine otter; local names for it include *nutria* (which usually means muskrat). The marine otter is much less well studied than the sea otter, so grad students take note: there's a great master's thesis still waiting to be written.

North American River Otter *Lontra canadensis*

Anybody remember a backyard toy from the sixties, the Slip 'N Slide? Plugged into a garden hose, it turned a summer day into a sheet of slippy, trippy fun. That's an otter's view of what life should be like: a careening Slip 'N Slide ride, with a bucket of minnows and crawdads waiting at the end. They can make their own slides out of mud or snow, and they can certainly catch their own perch, suckers, clams, frogs, and crawdads, but who doesn't like to dream about the small ways everyday life could be made better?

River otters are otters that like rivers (truth in advertising for once), and in California they're still common in the Northwest, along the Western Sierra, and in the Sacramento Delta. If they were present historically in the Colorado River along the California–Arizona border they were never very common, and they are not there now. In places like Redwood National Park they can mess about on the beach or coastal lagoons but are always smaller than sea otters and basically stick to fresh water. One way otters let us know they are among us is through their scat, or feces, which often includes the shells of crabs and crayfish, or a sparkle of fish scales.

Why don't they get cold when spending so much time in very chilly water? Size helps—they're over three feet long, including their thick tails, and adults weigh between ten and thirty pounds.

The main insulation, however, comes from tiny air bubbles trapped throughout an otter's dense fur. The nose and feet pads lose heat first, and no river otter can stay in frigid water indefinitely, but their fur is dense enough that they can be primarily (though not entirely) aquatic.

That same fur made them targets in the nineteenth and twentieth centuries. Otters in California and elsewhere were trapped for their pelts, making them locally extinct ("extirpated," to use the correct term). Trapping has been outlawed now for over fifty years, and slowly otters are returning to previous habitats. One citizen science initiative called the Otter Spotter program has helped document the river otter's return to almost all points of the San Francisco Bay. When combined with camera traps, field work, and roadkill analysis, the data reveal breeding populations in many Bay Area counties.

There has never been a day in my life when I was not in love.

—Edward Abbey

Welcome home, chaps. We've turned the Slip 'N Slide on just for you.

American Badger *Taxidea taxus*

Tejon Ranch on I-5 is named for this one (*tejón* is Spanish for "badger"), as are honey badgers in Africa; the American badger is a low-to-ground, bear-clawed, gray-backed, stripe-faced gopher chomper. It favors western grasslands from Canada to Mexico, and though it may not seem common, it manages to survive among us with surprising tenacity. Badgers live as close to L.A. as the Antelope Valley and the Santa Monica Mountains, as close to San Francisco as Mount Tamalpais, as close to Highway 101 as Santa Maria. In Europe, the badger looks similar to ours but is even heavier bodied and more boldly face striped.

In California, badgers can be found in agricultural fields, all types of prairie grassland, and even high desert steppes. What all badgers do is dig. They want holes to live in and squirrel and gopher colonies to dine on, so a place like Carrizo Plain National Monument is ideal. They are also found at Point Reyes and in the Great Basin section of California, plus in the Mojave National Preserve and at Camp Pendleton near San Diego. Contiguous blocks of intact landscape matter, and not just as viewsheds. In order to maintain enough territory for hunting its dispersed prey, a badger's home range is typically 2,000 acres, as opposed to a raccoon's (10 to 80 acres) or a chipmunk's (3 acres). Native Americans and early woodsmen alike were impressed by an unlikely partnership: sometimes a coyote and a badger will hunt together. One is a good chaser and pouncer, and one can dig like the dickens. Between them they are SEAL Team Six.

A running badger has a ground-hugging shimmy like a marmot's, but the two don't overlap in habitat and marmots never have a striped face. Not much eats badgers; their front paws call to mind Wolverine (the Marvel character as well as the forest mammal), and mountain lions don't come across badgers very often. Red-tailed hawks might hover over an at-work badger, hoping to grab any stray rodents the main digging misses, but since they weigh twenty-five pounds, not even a golden eagle can stoop an adult badger without giving it some thought first. For badgers, mountain lions are less worry than are roads, cars, dogs, and habitat fragmentation.

In fact, all perception is limited, no matter how acute your eyesight, how sharp the hearing, how sensitive the sense of touch. What we can take in is a partial rendering of the world. To go for a walk with a dog is enough to illustrate this principle.

—Mark Doty

Strange but true: badger fur once provided American and European men with the dense yet flexible bristles used in shaving brushes.

California Sea Lion and Steller Sea Lion

Zalophus californianus and *Eumetopias jubatus*

Is Brenda Hillman being mean or just accurate when she says in California "sea lions drape on rocks / like carpet samples"? Sea lions drape not just on rocks, but haul up on beaches, breakwaters, docks, buoys, and the sport decks of moored boats. On land they look a bit drunk, heads swaying and butts always a Slinky-jump behind, but once in the water sea lions slim down into efficiency personified. A flap-and-glide propulsion system and fast-as-a-speeding-bullet shape combine to make swimming as easy for sea lions as sending a text is for us.

Color varies from sleek black to suede blond depending on how wet or dry the animal is, depending on molt cycle, and depending on sex. Bull-necked males run darker than females and average about eight feet long; females average six feet and weigh two-thirds less. Head shape differs too, with males showing a steep bulge at the start of the forehead, a feature called the sagittal crest.

Most sea lions breed on the Channel Islands and on south to Mexico. After fending off rivals, dominant males hold territories that females enter and exit at will; these fiefdoms can extend from high on shore to far under the water. Pups are usually born midsummer a year later. If an El Niño episode happens to hit soon after, reduced fish stock causes the freshman class to struggle for survival. Emaciated pups that make it to mainland beaches from Channel Island rookeries often end up being taken in by rescue groups. Some make it; some don't. At the local scale, that feels (and is) tragic, but on the macro scale, sea lion populations thrive, and they are found along the entire Pacific coast and into the Gulf of Mexico. In the Galápagos, that kind is now listed as its own species, and there was a closely related third species found in Japan, but that one is now extinct. Three more sea lion species occur in the Southern Hemisphere.

Larger and found more northerly than the sea lion, the Steller sea lion (left) can be identified by the shape of its snout—shorter and broader in Steller; longer and more pointed in California.

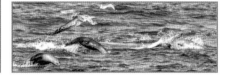

At the Farallon Islands off of San Francisco, California sea lions overlap with a northern species, the Steller sea lion. This kind may well deserve "stellar" performance ratings but is in fact named for eighteenth-century naturalist Georg Steller, the same person remembered in common names for a blue jay, a sea eagle, an eider duck, and an extinct thirty-foot manatee, the Steller's sea cow. You can tell a male Steller sea lion from a California sea lion by the face: a California sea lion has a snout like a German shepherd, but Steller sea lions are more compressed and bearlike, and unlike the California sea lion, the Steller sea lion doesn't have a sagittal crest.

Sea lions were once featured in shows at zoos, circuses, and aquariums, though the public's tolerance for trained-but-imprisoned wild animals has faded. These

You think dark is just one color, but it ain't. There're five or six kinds of black.
—Toni Morrison, Song of Solomon

days we would rather kayak with sea lions at Moss Landing or hear them barking in the middle of the night from our seaside hotel rooms. There's not yet a coffee mug with this slogan on it, but perhaps there should be: *A free seal is a happy seal.*

Northern Elephant Seal *Mirounga angustirostris*

One early fan of this book asked, "Oh, are you going to include those funny whale seals?" We are indeed, and the males do look like a cross between a beached whale and Jabba the Hutt, with a Jimmy Durante schnoz and a body that weighs more than two tons. Females and juveniles almost look like normal seals, though are still slob bodied and sausage nosed. (Odds are they think we look hideously ugly too, with our pointy faces and stick-figure postures.)

This is one that nearly didn't make it, since in the nineteenth century elephant seals were killed for their blubber, which was boiled down into lamp oil. Systematic hunting pushed them to the very pinprick of extinction. The population continues to recover at 6 percent a year, and now you can see them at Año Nuevo State Park, or from a pullout along Highway 1 just north of San Simeon. There is also a viewing area at Point Reyes, or, if you have your own boat, you can try the far side of San Miguel Island. You can find them off Baja and on the South Farallon Islands, and they are sometimes seen from whale-watching boats out of Monterey.

Appearance on land divides by sex-segregated shifts. They spend much of their time at sea but do come ashore to mate and to molt. Roughly speaking, female and juvenile seals molt from May through June and older males from July through August. Pups are born in December, January, and February. As the population continues to recover, you can see elephant seals in California almost every month of the year. A few even pretend they are harbor seals and haul out on Children's Cove in La Jolla.

When you do see an elephant seal, one thing you probably don't appreciate is the gold medal depths it can reach while hunting fifty different kinds of squid, skate, shark, and rockfish. On the beach they may look like a roll of dirty carpet that just fell off the back of a truck, but out at sea they can rival the exploits of Captain Nemo and the *Nautilus*—all-time records include one dive that went down 5,085 feet, and one male that stayed under for two hours. A sister species in the Southern Hemisphere, the southern elephant seal, has made even deeper dives. Even sperm whales are impressed.

Killing seals for oil may seem barbaric to us now, but one bull elephant seal could be turned into twenty-five gallons of oil, or in modern numbers, enough juice to run your iPhone for two or three years. In the nineteenth century, American whaling and sealing fleets comprised one of our largest (and most profitable) industries, and even though conditions on board ship were brutal, the ships also were multilingual and multiracial co-ops, with free health care and guaranteed profit sharing for all surviving hands.

The stars we are given.
The constellations we make.
—*Rebecca Solnit*

Luckily for us (and for the animals), in their ruthless efficiency, the sealers missed a few elephant seals here and there. If we want oil today, we can just frack the heck out of North Dakota to get it, leaving nature's other oil wells to doze the summer away in the shadow of Hearst Castle.

Harbor Seal _Phoca vitulina_

If these seals were horses they would be blue roans, grays, or buckskins. Color varies with how wet or dry the pelt is, and there can also be red ones if they're stained by iron oxide, but most harbor seals are some version of gray dappled with dark spots. In comparison, sea lions are always solidly brown, never speckled, and if seen close, sea lions have small but distinct ears. (Harbor seals do have ears, but hidden inside their heads.) Besides the color of their coats, you can also ID harbor seals by posture, since they often curve up like bananas when resting, as if they don't want to get their flippers wet. (They are probably just staying warm.) Another ID point is voice: sea lions go _arf arf arf_, but harbor seals are usually silent, though they can growl and hiss if threatened, and the pups have a mournful _kroo_ if mom gets too far away.

Harbor seals occur up and down the Pacific coast from Baja to Alaska and across to Japan, and also in the Maritimes of Canada, down the Atlantic side of the US, and across Europe up to the northernmost sites, where harbor seals dodge polar bears. In Europe, another name is the common seal—and it is indeed still relatively common, numbering maybe half a million worldwide. Since it lives a lot of places people do, conflicts sometimes arise. In La Jolla, a sandy cul-de-sac called Children's Cove has been the center of numerous lawsuits, as society tries to figure out if pretty little beaches are mostly for people, mostly for harbor seals, maybe a bit for both on alternating days, or perhaps beaches are just good places to build martial arts cages and let lawyers bash and claw to victory—may the largest briefcase win.

The seals of course just carry on eating fish, like the torpedo-shaped predators that they are. They also take squid and shellfish, weaving through the kelp forests with stealth and agility. Smaller than sea lions and also more strictly coastal, harbor seals average five to six feet and weigh two hundred to three hundred pounds. Killer whales and great white sharks hunt them. Most days harbor seals spend part of low tide resting on rocks or hauled up on shore, but they also can sleep underwater in communal rookeries called haul-downs. They come up to breathe and then sink back down to continue napping.

All seals are a kind of otter-bear that decided to return to the ancestral seas; even nonspecialists call them pinnipeds, a handy catchall term for seals, sea lions, elephant seals, and walruses. Pinniped skeletons reveal their terrestrial origins, including the presence of a tail—in an X-ray, most pinnipeds look like stretched out dogs who just happen to be wearing a sleeping bag for their Halloween costume.

Away from California, harbor seals can give birth on glacier ice,

What is a scientist after all? Just a curious man looking through a keyhole, the keyhole of nature, trying to know what's going on.

—Jacques-Yves Cousteau

or in Canada there's a freshwater form, the Ungava seal, that eats brook trout. Yet if we look at all the habitats and options, then look at the idyllic weather and attractive scenery of La Jolla, it's no wonder the seals want to take over Children's Cove. For most of us, that is a great blessing, since even when the beach is closed for pupping, there's an adjacent causeway you can stroll along, and no matter how large or oohing-and-aahing the crowds, the seals are happy to share the view, the fresh air, and the infinite wonder of life's continuing miracle.

Gray Whale *Eschrichtius robustus*

Gray whales are the winter whales off California, commuting up and down the coast twice yearly as they go from the feeding grounds in Alaska and even farther north and back down to the breeding lagoons of Baja. This is a 10,000-mile roundtrip journey, and late southbound whales pass the early northbound ones off the coast of Southern California; February is peak time. A splinter sect figures that Point Reyes is as far north as they need to go, and that group summers in the Gulf of the Farallones.

Seen well, this is a rather blotchy, simple whale, forty to fifty feet long with a ridgeline of knuckles down the back (no dorsal fin) and crusty patches of Jackson Pollock barnacles. Those are just there for the ride: rather than latch on to a rock and let the waves bring the food to them, gray whale barnacles use the forward motion of the whale to bring them to the food. The whales strain food from the water too, using a five-foot tongue and a dense comb of baleen plates, but unlike barnacles, they feed more actively. One method involves plowing the soft mud of the seafloor to hoover up worms, mollusks, and invertebrates. A bottom-foraging whale leaves twenty-foot trenches in the seabed and trails behind a plume of mud. Collectively, this stirs the bottom of the soup pot very helpfully, as other birds and fish follow the whale close behind, chasing leftovers. Gray whales also feed at the surface, taking krill, crabs, and bait fish, or they poke around in the kelp, slurping shrimp. Contrary to prior claims, they do not fast during migration, though they do slowly lose weight.

This is a surprisingly agile beast: grays can spy-hop to have a look around, and while they're not as show-offy as humpbacks, they too can lunge and splash, with loud breaches that maybe knock off parasites (like whale lice), maybe tell others that they are around, or maybe just feel fun. If you were to chase one in a boat and try to harpoon it, that agility would be formidable: whalers called them devil fish because the mothers fought back fiercely when the whalers killed their babies in the breeding lagoons. Now they tolerate being petted by tourists from boats in Baja, just showing that if you are willing to be nice to the world, the world usually is nice right back.

Unlike their oceanic cousins, gray whales are a nearshore species, staying along coasts and around islands. That means dead ones wash ashore more often than other species, and in California, coastal tribes once ate fresh whale meat or smoked it for later; bones were used to make tools, grave markers, housing struts, and (at least in

If you free yourself from the conventional reaction to a quantity like a million years, you free yourself a bit from the boundaries of human time. And then in a way you do not live at all, but in another way you live forever.
—John McPhee

one village) charms against rattlesnakes. Does that work? Apparently so, since for many years my daughter had a plastic aquarium whale she kept in her hiking pack. In all the time she had it, she was not bothered by snakes even once.

Humpback Whale *Megaptera novaeangliae*

This is our splashiest, most common summer whale, visible some days even from shore. As whales go, it's a midsized model—not a record-breaker, but at fifty feet long, still plenty big. Expect it via boats out of Monterey; a typical August trip will tally at least a dozen, though there are lucky days when your binoculars pick whales on all sides of the boat, all the way out to the blurry edge of the horizon. Birders know that means food is abundant and sooty shearwaters and black-footed albatrosses won't be far away.

Experts identify whales (or pretend to identify whales) by shape and location of the dorsal fin and by the shape of the exhaled spout. The humpback has a ridged, "two-step" back with a small but distinct fin, plus a bushy, diffuse blow. Compared to other whales it has long, flexible "arms" (pectoral fins): their size and blotchy white color contribute to ID. Usual behavior might be a dozen surface breaths and then a tail-waving "catch ya later" signal as it dives to feed. Seeing tail flukes means time to be patient: they can dive to six hundred feet and stay under for thirty minutes (though five or ten is more typical). Often two or three humpbacks will be paired up to feed for the day and when seen from the side, their synchronized surfacing recalls the coiled humps of a sea serpent, even down to a crenellated row of Loch Ness Monster fins.

Humpbacks can be divided into populations based on geography. Our humpbacks feed on anchovies and krill in summer and fall, eating up to a ton per day, then go south to Mexico and Central America in winter. The California humpback is the same species you may have seen in Maui, though that population mostly feeds in Alaska in the summer, then migrates (at one or two miles an hour) back to Hawai'i to mate and give birth. Another Pacific population feeds in the Aleutian Islands and migrates to Japan. There are Southern Hemisphere groups as well, along with humpbacks in the Atlantic and Indian oceans: it is more cosmopolitan than James Bond.

These whales are the show-offs of the cetacean world, with a remarkable agility for something that weighs as much as two rush-hour buses. Their behavior is often more *lucha libre* than finicky ballet, and while their pounding splashes, surface-ripping lunges, and whole-body breaches make for great photo ops, much of it still puzzles scientists. Just what are they doing? As with gray whales, maybe a really satisfying belly flop knocks parasites loose (which seagulls pick up afterwards), while maybe a vigorous tail throw says, "Hey guys, wait up!" They don't seem to mind boats and once in a while do a big heave so close that the splash drenches the passengers.

Humpbacks often feed in pairs. When they surface near one another, they look like coils of the same animal—it was perhaps this sight that inspired the myth of sea monsters.

We know that they have big brains and complex social interactions, but other specifics elude us. Drones have sampled twenty-five species of microbes in one whale breath, so there must be an interior ecology we have yet to learn about, while their complex vocalizations sidle up disturbingly close to most dictionary definitions of language. As author Christopher Moore says, "Regardless of its purpose, the humpback-whale song is the most complex piece of nonhuman composition on earth. Whether it's art, prayer, or booty call, [it] is an amazing thing to experience firsthand."

I would rather have questions that can't be answered than answers that can't be questioned.
—Richard Feynman

Killer whales try to take the calves, and a few humpbacks die each year from ship strikes, but in general things seem okay. We can all be glad they are no longer are hunted most places (though a few are still taken in Greenland) and that populations seem to be increasing. Guesstimates put the Pacific population at 20,000. Some days it seems that almost all of them are one place: Monterey Bay.

Blue Whale *Balaenoptera musculus*

Start with the name: "blue" for the color of its immense and magical body when it is lingering just beneath the surface of the sea—yet not a drab blue, like old jeans or dull paint, but a luminous, "How can water catch on fire?" kind of blue. And "whale," a word going past *Beowulf* to the earliest origins of the English language. Yet neither term explains the shock and awe of seeing one in the wild. Numbers do not help much either. How long is it? Up to 98 feet, though 80 is more usual. How deep do they dive? Maybe 1,600 feet, though a much smaller cetacean, Cuvier's beaked whale, has been recorded at 10,000 feet, so probably we do not know the full stats for this part yet. How much do they eat? Up to 40 million krill a day, weighing a total of 4 tons. Krill are basically shrimp, and they turn the whale's poop bright pink, a bloom of effluent that stinks like a fifty-fifty mix of rotting fish and burning tires.

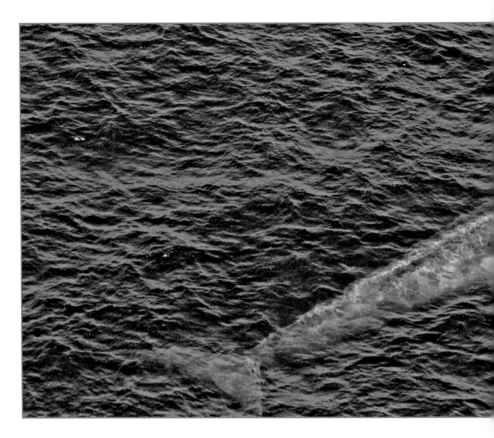

We look for blue whales in summer off of the Monterey coast. Experts name it at a distance not by size but by the shape of its diffuse, off-axis spout. Once up close, everybody on the boat can agree: this is one big animal. The head breaks the surface with a quick and bushy blow and next comes the back, glistening in the sunlight as the whale rolls through the rest of its pre-dive arc. We know to expect a dorsal fin and maybe a flash of flukes if it's about to sound for a dive. Only the back keeps going...and going...and going...until you think, "Will this animal never end?" Finally, there's a modest dorsal fin stuck on the far end like an afterthought, and if we do see tail flukes, that means it's time to be patient since the whale has probably gone down for ten or twenty minutes. Just after they dive, the surface of the sea shows a footprint (as it's called)—a dome of stilled water contrasting with the rest of the more stirred-up, wind-chopped surface.

Which is bigger, a blue whale or a dinosaur? Go with whale, since any of the fossil contenders for mega-mega-saurus would need to be much lighter than a whale in order not to collapse under its own mass. If you want to grow to be truly immense, live in water.

As for the legacy of whaling, yes, these animals were hunted—brutally, ruthlessly, relentlessly. There were factory ships and grenade-tipped harpoons. The

more we learn about cetacean social structures, the worse whaling seems. One journal study proved that whales mourn their dead, staying with deceased offspring for days; other studies estimate that whaling was responsible for population declines of 90 or even 99 percent.

Now we are marginally more enlightened, and hunting has nearly ended; slowly, world populations have begun to recover. After feasting on krill along the West Coast, blue whales migrate to the waters of Costa Rica to breed and give birth. How do they get there? Whales navigate the world using sound (blue whales sing long, slow, thousand-mile songs—too low for humans to hear), a magnetic compass, and internal star charts.

The usual fact—"fact" in air quotes—is that a blue whale's heart is the size of a car. It's not, but it would pretty much fill up the average hot tub nicely, and it does weigh 400 pounds. When you see a blue whale your own heart swells up just about that big too, and you think the day can't get much better—until, of course, you see one more.

The sea, once it casts its spell, holds one in its net of wonder forever.

—Jacques-Yves Cousteau

Dolphins Delphinidae

If seals and sea lions are pinnipeds and if the larger whales are called cetaceans, what word should we use to describe California's two dozen dolphin and porpoise species? We sure have a lot of them, measured by overall numbers (3,500 common dolphins in one pod) and by the mix of species possible on any given boat trip (up to five or more on a good day in Monterey). You can see them from shore, and on the calmest, stillest, foggiest winter mornings, even *hear* them from shore, as they exhale with a little pop-top-on-a-can-of-soda *spiff* of breath. Instead of the Golden State, a better name might have been the "whale, dolphin, and porpoise state." Somebody please go and tell the coastal chambers of commerce to make the switch.

Dolphins live in social units called pods and our species are all oceanic, although in the Amazon and parts of Asia there are freshwater dolphins adapted to life in rivers—and in North America, the harbor porpoise can indeed be found in marinas and harbors. Counting the mega-dolphins (killer whales and false killer whales and pilot whales) plus the closely related porpoise clan, there are about fifty dolphin species worldwide. In California, colors range from black and white (Dall's porpoises, northern right whale dolphins) to dark gray (bottlenose dolphins) to hourglass swirls of pearl, cream, and tan (common dolphins).

Long-beaked common dolphin.

Risso's dolphin.

Long-beaked common dolphin.

Elsewhere in the world there are even pink dolphins; it feels unfair that we don't have those here.

Most dolphins bow ride, meaning they like to race up alongside a moving ship and surf the pressure wave pushed ahead by the boat. Dozens jockey into position, and as one peels off, another sprints up to take its place—you can almost hear them shouting "ya-*hoo!*" Looking down from the deck of the boat you can see them racing in the water and you feel like you're flying right there with them. (You know you're having an amazing marine mammal experience when you need a wide-angle lens—not a telephoto—to get the best shots.)

You can also see dolphins from the beach, as there is a coastal form of bottlenose dolphin which hunts very close to shore—so close to shore that sometimes you can see the entire body in the transparent water of backlit waves. The bottlenose dolphin is the "Flipper" species, with the enigmatic smile and distinct dorsal

Bottlenose dolphin.

fin that we know from television and movies. Although found worldwide, different populations specialize in nearshore or offshore hunting. Offshore bottlenose dolphins in California can be found at sea well past the continental shelf, while the nearshore groups range from Baja to Monterey (and, rarely, San Francisco Bay), and are the ones that can even be seen from a seaside restaurant in Malibu.

No matter how politely one says it, we owe our existence to the farts of blue-green algae.
—Diane Ackerman

The Risso's dolphin or grampus has a shape similar to the bottlenose dolphin but shows more white and gray (bottlenose is usually darker), and most individuals have scars from the sharp-beaked squids that they hunt, and from sparring with rivals. Watch for them on Monterey Bay whale-watching boat trips.

Because of California's rich cetacean diversity, only a sample of all the amazing species can be included here. For those who feel that even six or seven dolphin pictures are never enough, we too agree with you, but luckily there is an ocean full of dolphins and porpoises, and all we have to do is go and look.

Killer Whale *Orcinus orca*

Black and white and with a surfboard-sized dorsal fin, a killer whale looks like Shamu, which is to say it looks like a cross between a penguin and a nuclear submarine. The Inuit name is *aarluk* ("kills everything") and collectively they do take on anything that bobs, floats, dives, or swims, from squid to polar bears to other whales. A whale-watching boat near the Farallon Islands once videotaped a killer whale fighting a great white shark. (The killer whale won.) We should note, however, that there has never been a proven attack on humans in the wild.

Killer whales are also called orcas, a word that comes to us from French and once meant "sea monster," unless it comes from Roman mythology and means kingdom of the dead. On paper they're not whales but dolphins, but that's like saying a man-eating tiger is basically just a very ambitious lynx. They generally live in social units called pods, a group of two to fifteen animals governed by a senior matriarch who may live to be over a hundred. Pods hunt cooperatively and share food. Like humans (and pilot whales), female killer whales do go through menopause, probably so the daughters and granddaughters in the same pod can raise young successfully, since a nursing mother orca has to eat up to 40 percent more food than her sisters and brothers. (Most mammals do not stop reproducing in old age, and a grandma elephant still can bear young.)

Pods specialize in one kind of prey and either roam to find it or stay centered in one territory, like the salmon-hunting orcas of Puget Sound. Because the killer whale is found worldwide and all of them look roughly the same, initially it was thought to be one species. Closer study breaks it down into more distinct units. These units (tribes? clans?) are not different species, not exactly, yet they might be different species inexactly. Perhaps we are seeing speciation happen in real time? The groups differ by dialect, hunting strategy, and prey choice, and if they never mingle genetically, that is one definition of what makes a species a species. Follow-

There is beauty, heartbreaking beauty, everywhere.

—Edward Abbey

ing this new research, there seem to be at least three groups: the residents, the transients, and the far-from-shorers. It may be even more complicated than that; don't be surprised to see multiple new orca species proposed in the next few years, announcements that will in turn be counterargued.

For now, let's just call them all killer whales. Where can you go to see them? Since they follow gray whales north from Baja (hoping to harry the calves), Point Vicente in early spring is a good vantage point. In Monterey Bay the season starts a bit later, and in April and May there are boat trips dedicated just to looking for them. Yet orcas come and go according to whale time, not human time, and off our coasts any month can provide surprises, gifts, sightings, excitement.

The fact is, however often one goes out, it is impossible to be blasé about killer whales. Do we want to identify with them as fellow apex predators? Or is it more about the thrill that comes from being close to something larger, fiercer, more unknowable than ourselves?

No matter what the source of the attraction, we all like knowing that they are out there. Nature can sustain our imaginations even when we can't experience it directly: some days—not always, but sometimes—the thought of such an awe-inspiring creature can be pleasure enough.

Acknowledgments

This book had help from many sources. The author would like to thank the following spotters, reviewers, companions, and dream catchers:

Karen Baker, Bruce Bartrug, Blackfin Joe, Jean-Michel Bompar, Jared Burton, Paul Carter, Carol Chambers, Andy Crosby, Sally Crosby, Vladimir Dinets, Tanya Espinosa, Holly Faithfull, Kelly Fernandez, José Gabriel Martínez-Fonseca, Jonathan Franzen, Kristin Friedrich, Joan Fry, Kate Gale, Charles Goodrich, Jon Hall, Curtis Hart, John Haubrich, Lila Higgins, Abbey Hood, Amber Hood, Fred Hood, Matthew Jaffe, Morten Joergensen, Marcelo Marcos, Chet McGaugh, Alex Meyer, Bill Noble, Greg Pauly, Fiona Reid, Micah Riegner, Matt Ritter, Venkat Sakar, Phil Telfer, Jerry Ting, Bill Vaughn, Betsy Winchell, John Wright, and Cal Yorke.

A very special thank you to wildlife biologist Miguel Ordeñana.

Last but never least, the author waves his hat and whoops in a circle to thank the terrific staff at Heyday: Emmerich Anklam, Mariko Conner, Briony Everroad, Ashley Ingram, Diane Lee, Christopher Miya, Steve Wasserman, and editor-to-the-stars Gayle Wattawa.

Photo Credits

Adobe Stock: 47, 48 (bottom left), 54, 106 (bottom), 133, 137–38

Jean-Michel Bompar: 43, 44 (all except bottom), 45, 46, 48 (top)

Tyler Campbell/USDA: 53

Paul Carter: xxvi, 2 (bottom), 6, 7, 11 (top left, bottom right), 13 (inset), 14, 15, 18 (top left, top right), 24, 26 (top), 30 (top right), 34, 37, 38 (bottom), 39, 59 (top left), 61, 62 (top), 74 (right), 75, 90 (left, bottom), 115 (all), 116 (top), 117, 118 (inset), 122 (all), 123 (top), 125, 140, 141 (bottom), 143, 145

José G. Martínez-Fonseca: 2 (top), 22, 49, 76, 129

Jon Hall/Mammalwatching.com: 119

Curtis Hart: 31 (inset), 92

John Haubrich: 9 (top), 19, 20 (top), 28, 29, 31, 40 (all), 50, 55, 58, 59 (top right, bottom), 60, 62 (bottom left, right), 63–65, 66 (middle), 69 (bottom), 81 (top), 82, 84 (bottom), 91 (right), 92 (inset), 93, 95 (all), 101 (inset), 108 (bottom right), 109 (bottom left, right), 120 (top), 135 (bottom), 150

Jared Hobbs/Alamy Stock Photo: 104 (inset)

Abbey Hood: 161

Charles Hood: cover, ii, xi (middle, bottom), xii–xxv, xxvii, 1, 4, 5, 8, 10, 11 (bottom left), 12, 13, 16, 17, 18 (bottom left, bottom right), 21 (all), 23, 25, 26 (middle), 27, 30 (all except top right), 32, 33, 35 (all), 36 (all), 38 (top, inset), 41 (all), 42 (all), 53 (inset), 57 (top), 66 (bottom right), 67, 68 (top, bottom left), 69 (top), 71, 72, 73 (top), 74 (top left), 77 (all), 78 (all), 88, 89, 90 (right), 91 (inset), 97 (inset), 98, 100, 101, 105, 106 (inset), 108 (top left), 113 (middle), 116 (bottom left, bottom right), 120 (bottom left), 123 (bottom left, bottom right), 127, 128 (middle, bottom), 132 (all), 134, 135 (top), 136 (all), 141 (top), 144 (bottom), 152, 159, 162

Fred Hood: x, xi (top), 26 (bottom), 51 (right), 56, 57 (bottom), 66 (top left, top right, bottom left), 68 (bottom right), 70, 79, 80, 81 (inset), 83, 84 (top), 85, 86, 94, 96, 99, 102, 104 (top), 106 (top left, top right), 107, 108 (top right, bottom left), 110, 112, 113 (all except middle), 114, 120 (bottom right), 162–163

Morten Joergensen/NozoMojo.com: 121, 123 (bottom center), 124, 126, 130, 131, 137 (all), 142, 144 (top, middle)

Leopardinatree/istock: 20 (bottom)

Alexander Meyer: 44 (bottom), 48 (bottom right)

Natural History Museum of Los Angeles County: 3

A bull elk opens his mouth in a flehmen response, checking the air for rivals.

David Lehmann tracking mandrills in Gabon, West Africa.

Further Resources

Most large national parks in the United States have mammal lists available on their websites; smaller parks might too, but you sometimes need to ask in person at the visitor center. Another great tool is the iNaturalist database, which you can search by region, park name, taxa (by amphibians and birds, for example), or other filters.

To learn how to tell a red fox from an arctic fox, Fiona Reid's *Peterson Field Guide to Mammals of North America* is first among equals. It pairs well with Vladimir Dinets's *Peterson Field Guide to Finding Mammals in North America*.

In a category of its own is mammalwatching.com, a free site that provides a forum for sharing trip reports and taxonomy updates for species and locations worldwide. Every week it seems that its contributors are crisscrossing exotic terrain, seeing snow leopards in Tibet or counting bats in Brazil. If you were thinking, say, of a long weekend in Azerbaijan and wanted tips on finding Persian gazelles, this is the place to start. But North America is well represented too, and one premise of the site is that for every animal, from flying squirrel to pygmy hippo, there's a piece of forest that is the best place to try—we just need to figure out where it is.

Index

A

Ackerman, Diane 75
Aesop xi
Alaska xvii, 19, 27, 84, 85, 93, 97, 111, 114, 127,
    131, 134
albatross, black-fronted 133
albino xx
Aleutian Islands 134
Angeles Crest 49, 61, 62
Año Nuevo State Park 125
Antelope Valley 39, 56, 119
Anza, Juan Bautista de 61
Anza-Borrego State Park xxii, 24, 61, 91
Arcata 79
Audubon, John James 30
Australia 8, 72, 75

B

badger, American xxiii, 59
badger, European, 119
Baja xvi, 23, 75, 114, 125, 127, 131, 142, 145
Bakersfield 92
Baldwin Hills 85
Bass, Rick 98
bat, California leaf-nosed 75
bat, greater fishing xvi
bat, hoary 78
bat, pallid xiii, 78
bat, spotted 77-78
bat, western mastiff 78
bats xxiv, xxv, xxvii, xx, 75-78
Bateman, Robert 30
bear, American black xix, xx, xxvii, 81, 93-95
bear, brown 97
bear, grizzly xix, 35, 63, 83, 84, 94, 96-98, 111
beaver, American 31-33, 108
beaver, European 31
Big Bear 74, 98
Big Sur 115
Bishop 93
bobcat xx, 81, 92, 107-109
Bodega Bay 33
Bodie xxv, 21
Bolinas xxvi
Botta, Paolo Emilio 35
Brandberg Mountains xii
burro, feral 71-74

C

cacomistle 101
California Floristic Province 12
camel, feral xix
Camp Pendleton 119
Canada xvii, 83, 108, 119, 127, 129
caracal 109
Carrizo Plain National Monument 37, 40, 59, 119
cat, feral xix, xx, 105-106
Catalina Island 23, 90, 115
Central Valley 56
cetacean 140
Channel Islands 23, 49, 89, 104, 108, 121
Chauvet Cave xi
chickadee, chestnut-backed xxi
Children's Cove 127, 129
Chile 116
China 48
chipmunk, least 30
chipmunk, Uinta 30
chipmunks 25, 28-30, 69
Chuckwalla Mountains 56
Colorado River 31, 33, 40, 117
condor, California 35
coquí frog xi
Costa Rica 139
cottontail, desert 10-12, 91
cottontail, mountain 12
cougar 111
coydog 79, 81
coyote xix, xxi, 11, 12, 23, 79-81, 85, 91-92, 99,
    103, 108, 119
Custer, George Armstrong 40

D

Death Valley National Park xi, xviii, 7, 39, 49,
    74, 91, 111
deer, black-tailed 67
deer, mule xviii, xx, xxi, xxiii, xxv, 53, 55, 67-69,
    108, 111
deer, red 65
deer, white-tailed 42, 67
deer mouse, North American 40-42
deer mice 40-42, 45
Del Norte Coast Redwoods State Park xi
Del Norte County 33
Denali National Park 84

The Mexican long-tongued bat usually pollinates cactus and agave, but they love hummingbird feeders too.

About the Author

Poet and essayist Charles Hood is the author of *A Californian's Guide to the Birds among Us* (Heyday) and also collaborated with the Natural History Museum of Los Angeles County on *Wild L.A.: Explore the Amazing Nature in and around Los Angeles* (Timber Press). A reformed birder, he now is trying to ease up on his world mammal list. Charles lives and teaches in the Mojave Desert; his wife, Abbey, keeps a mammal list as well, though only of the species she has seen and he has not.

Photo by Abbey Hood.

Hiking, with or without wildlife sightings, is always a grand way to spend a morning.